D. Caroline Coile, Ph.D.

# Jack Russell Terriers

Everything About
Housing, Care, Nutrition, Breeding,
and Health Care

Filled with Full-color Photographs

Illustrations by Tana Hakanson

# 2 CONTENTS

# THE WILD HUNT

Scene stealer of stage shows and horse shows, too cute, too smart, and far too appealing for its own good, to see a Jack Russell Terrier is to want one. And therein lies the problem. Because, for all of its appeal as an irascible fun-loving scamp, the Jack Russell Terrier was born to hunt. These dogs seek out trouble. That's part of their appeal, but also part of the difficulty of owning them.

To understand the Jack Russell Terrier you must accept one fact: This is a dog driven by an overpowering instinctive urge to explore and hunt. To understand why this urge is so well developed in today's Jack Russells, you must delve into the story of the Jack Russells of yesterday.

## Hunting High and Low

Many breeds have an ancient and mysterious origin—the Jack Russell Terrier is not one of them. The Jack Russell Terrier (JRT) originated in large part from the dedicated efforts of Parson John (Jack) Russell (known as "The Sporting Parson") of Devonshire, England.

### John Russell's Terrier

While a student at Oxford, Russell often abandoned his studies in favor of fox hunting, a pastime to which his locale (if not his finances) allowed him ample access. Although fox hunting

*The Jack Russell Terrier's history is intertwined with horses and hounds.*

is most often identified with Foxhounds, every pack also included small terriers that could bolt a fox that had gone to ground so the hunt could continue. Such terriers were extremely important members of the hunt; after all, the success of the entire affair depended upon the tenacity, courage, intelligence, and athleticism of these dogs. It was such a terrier that John Russell wanted very badly. In 1819 the answer came from an unlikely source: a milkman who owned a terrier such as John Russell had only dreamed about. Russell acquired the female, named Trump, who went on to become the matriarch of the breed that now bears the Parson's name. Trump was described as being about the size of a "vixen fox," with a thick, close, slightly wiry coat, predominantly white with a patch of dark tan over each ear and eye and a dot of color on the root of her tail.

Although Trump is the acknowledged matriarch of the breed, no records remain as to what other dogs went into the recipe for Jack Russell Terriers. It is usually assumed, however, that they included local rough-coated and predominantly white terriers. Rough-coated dogs were the exception at the time, and these same dogs are also considered to be the foundation stock for modern wirehaired Fox Terriers.

After he was ordained, Russell moved to Devon where the countryside was open and rolling but punctuated by many badger holes in which a fox could hole up. Here he selected terriers that could trot behind the horses for hours, keep up with the hounds running at full

clip on the scent, and still have the stamina to enter a hole and bark at and work the fox until it fled. Russell also bred Foxhounds, and his bloodlines became well respected throughout the region, as did Russell himself. Russell was adored by his parishioners, who allowed him every freedom to pursue his passion for hunting, even when it interfered with his parochial duties.

John Russell's interest in dogs led him also to become one of the founders of England's Kennel Club, perhaps the most influential dog registration body in the world, and the organization most responsible for the sport of showing purebred dogs in conformation competitions. Although John Russell judged Fox Terriers in conformation in 1874, he never once exhibited his own Jack Russell Terriers at a conformation show. No doubt he preferred to spend his spare time in the field watching his dogs hunt foxes, not trophies, and he continued his love affair with the hunt until his last

*The early Jack Russell Terriers were primarily white, about the size of a female fox, and with a build to enable them to run long and hard as part of the fox hunting pack.*

year of life, in 1883. At the time of his death he had been breeding his strain of working terriers for 65 years.

# Confirmation of Conformation

In the latter half of the 19th century and early half of the 20th century, a canine revolution was taking place—a revolution that the Jack Russell Terrier somehow managed to miss. During those years, conformation dog shows were becoming fashionable, and purebred dogs, registered with The Kennel Club, were the vogue. Perhaps because fox hunters already had hound packs that had accomplished great acclaim, or perhaps because they were just too busy having fun in the field, they and their dogs remained apart from the dog show scene.

## Fields Rather than Rings

The tradition of proving Jack Russell Terriers in the field rather than in the ring has remained intact for well over a century. This emphasis upon field ability over conformation aspects is at the heart of what makes a Jack Russell Terrier different from most other modern breeds of dog.

Not only did most JRT proponents traditionally reject the idea of showing their dogs, but they also vehemently opposed official recognition of their breed by multibreed dog registra-

*Jack Russells had to have the mind and body to go anywhere the fox went.*

tion bodies such as The Kennel Club in England or the American Kennel Club (AKC) in the United States. They were opposed not only because of the emphasis these organizations place upon conformation dog shows, but also because these are purely pedigree-based registries. Any dog whose parents are registered with that organization is itself eligible for registration, no matter what the quality of that individual dog is. As the JRT is first and foremost a working terrier, its advocates consider evidence of pure breeding to be secondary to evidence of hunting ability and good health.

## The Most Popular Mutt in the World

The Jack Russell Terrier has been called "the most popular mutt in the world," referencing its frequent crosses to a smorgasbord of terrier breeds. This, coupled with the practice

*Short-legged, also called English Jack Russell Terriers, are extremely popular and have a special appeal.*

enough to squeeze into a burrow, plucky enough to face a snarling fox at close range, and ferocious enough to scare the fox out. Its job was to bark at the fox, not kill it.

## A Shorter-legged Terrier

In the early 1900s, the British countryside became crisscrossed with barbed wire fencing, aiding the decline of riding to the hounds. In addition, the rockier countryside of northwestern England near the Scottish border was not conducive to mounted hunting. A new type of fox hunter emerged who wanted a dog that would be an ally to a man on foot. Thus, a shorter-legged, slower, but scrappier terrier, whose job was to actually dispatch the fox, was favored, and the JRT was interbred with such dogs. The tough, short-legged result was also an excellent ratter and badger hunter, activities more readily accessible to the common man. But was it really a Jack Russell Terrier?

## The Real JRT

The stage was set for a heated debate. Which is the proper and true JRT: the traditional longer-legged dog said to be favored by the Parson himself (sometimes referred to as the Parson Jack Russell Terrier), or the shorter-legged dog dominating the breed in more recent times (sometimes referred to as the English Jack Russell Terrier)? In fact, the longer-legged JRT is considered to be the true breed representative by the AKC and the Jack Russell Terrier Club of America (JRTCA), whereas the

of interbreeding with exceptional hunting JRTs often lacking proof of pure JRT breeding, cause many people to call JRTs a strain, rather than a breed, of dog. Again, the emphasis upon ability over looks has led to a strain that varies considerably in type and size from dog to dog, a situation that creates some consternation among judges at conformation shows. JRTs come in different coat types, body sizes, and leg lengths, with height being a point of contention among many present-day breeders.

# The Long and the Short of It

The JRT was originally bred not to kill the fox, but to cause it to bolt from any hiding place so that the fox hunt could continue. Thus, it had to be fast enough to run with the hounds, small

English Jack Russell Terrier Club Alliance (EJRTCA) embraces the shorter-legged dogs. The earliest breed standard, written in 1904, called for a longer-legged dog, although some subsequent standards of different JRT associations allowed for a greater range of heights that encompassed the shorter-legged dogs.

# Join the Club!

The Parson Jack Russell Terrier Club was founded in England in 1914, and advocated the longer-legged "Parson" JRT. The JRT Club of Great Britain was formed much later, and used a standard that allowed for a wider range in height, including a shorter (but not dwarf-type) JRT. In America, the JRTCA also advocated a wider range in size. Both the JRT Club of Great Britain and the JRTCA were adamantly opposed to JRT recognition by any all-breed registry. In contrast, the Jack Russell Terrier Breeder's Association (JRTBA) in America favored the more restrictive standard for a longer-legged dog, as well as recognition by the AKC. The differences in standards and opinions regarding registration set the stage for a serious disagreement regarding the best future for the breed. In 1991 the English Kennel Club recognized the (British) Parson JRT. In America, the JRTBA, now called the Jack Russell Terrier Association of America (JRTAA), worked toward and achieved AKC acceptance. In 1998 the AKC admitted the JRT into the Miscellaneous Class, the first step toward regular AKC registration. In one of the fastest recent transitions of any breed through the Miscellaneous Class, the AKC admitted the

*Jack Russell Terriers are still a familiar sight around stables.*

JRT as a regular member of the Terrier group as of April 1, 2000.

## Club Competition

Unfortunately, the disagreement about the best way to serve the breed created a rift among JRT supporters and a lack of unification that can only hurt the breed. The JRTCA will not accept members who register or compete with their dogs through any multibreed registry, including the AKC and the UKC (United Kennel Club). Yet these registries offer more than conformation shows; they sponsor obedience, earth dog, and agility competitions that offer a fun way for owners to interact with their dogs. The JRTCA also offers these competitions, but they may not be as readily available

*The Jack Russell's fate is at a crossroads, pulled by both its traditional hunting heritage and its new job as pet and show dog.*

*Despite their irresistible stuffed dog appearance, the JRT is full of vim and vigor, and ready to raise havoc.*

in all parts of the country. Thus, JRT pet owners who simply want to enjoy their dogs are forced to make a decision about which registry to participate in, and to subsequently limit their participation to either the JRTCA or the AKC (and other all-breed clubs).

## Safeguarding the JRT

JRT advocates may disagree on the methods of best serving the breed, but there is one thing they do agree on—the JRT must be safeguarded to preserve its health, working instinct, and temperament, and it must be cautiously promoted lest it be placed with new owners who are not prepared to deal with the rambunctious and unique nature of the breed. Today, most JRTs find fulfilling lives serving the most important function any dog can—that of companion. The breed has enjoyed immense popularity in England for many years, and is rapidly gaining an almost cult-like following in America and elsewhere. The JRT is traditionally popular with the "horse set," no doubt in part because it is right at home accompanying the well turned-out hunter. It is a popular co-star of television shows, movies, and commercials, and this exposure, combined with the dog's saucy expression, humorous antics, and intelligent nature no doubt will continue to win more people over to this pert little breed. Long-time aficionados worry, however, that with such popularity comes the danger of careless breeding, overpopulation, exploitation, and poor placement of pups. For a breed that has survived over a century virtually unchanged, there is a dangerous crossroad

ahead. This breed is definitely not suited for everyone, and an incompatible match of dog and owner can spell a lifetime of shared unhappiness, or—far too often—a trip to the pound.

Too many people acquire a dog with the assumption that all breeds act the same. They do not. The very reason that different breeds were initially created stemmed from differences in behavior, not looks. Dogs were selected for their propensity to trail, point, retrieve, herd, protect, or even cuddle, with physical attributes often secondary to behavioral. More than most breeds, with its long history of selection based upon function, the JRT is a prime example. The JRT was selected to hunt by investigating, running, digging, and barking. Don't get a Jack Russell Terrier and ask it to act like a lapdog. It's simply not its nature.

# BODY AND SOUL

If an irresistible dog was ever created, it is the Jack Russell. With its impish face and clever antics, it seems the ideal pet for a person with a sense of adventure. It is. Add to this its Hollywood exposure, and it seems the JRT is the ideal dog for just about anyone and anything. It's not. Jack Russells are the perfect dogs for a small group of people who have the time, energy, facilities, and sense of humor to make them ideal. Most people do not.

## Temperament

Do you want a dog that will stay at your side on a walk, sleep in your lap for hours, and jump to obey your every command? Then you sure don't want a Jack Russell Terrier. Over 100 years of selection for working ability has produced a dog that loves to hunt.

✔ These dogs need to be bold, energetic, inquisitive, and relentless.

✔ Because the JRT's hunting style is not based upon following the hunter's directions (as it is in many sporting breeds, for example), they need to be independent and self-directed.

✔ They must be tough and tenacious in the face of adversity (even if that adversity is their owner telling them *"No!")*.

✔ They must be untiring in order to follow the fox over great distances (as any owner knows who has ever tried to catch a runaway JRT).

*The traditional JRT is high on spirit and high on leg.*

✔ They must bark with vigor and stamina (much to the next door neighbor's dismay).

✔ They must be willing, indeed, anxious, to seek out quarry and follow it underground.

Allowed to roam the neighborhood, the JRT feels compelled to range far afield and may not return for days, or at all; in fact, some JRTs have been found ensconced underground after being missing for days, unwilling to leave their quarry at any cost. Left alone in the yard, they will dig in search of moles, worms, and other buried treasure.

Everyone wants an intelligent dog, but few people realize that it is often much easier to live with a dumb dog than a smart one, especially when that intelligence is combined with independence. The JRT is an intelligent, independent dog.

JRTs tend to be leaders, and should be obedience trained so that they accept you as leader. Give a JRT an inch, and it will likely take several miles. This doesn't mean they need to be "shown who's boss" with force—just a consistent gentle but firm hand.

### The More Terriers the Merrier?

There are certain advantages, and disadvantages, to having more than one dog. Two dogs are twice the fun of one, without being twice the work—unless they fight. Terriers are notorious for quarreling with each other, but JRTs are bred to get along with other members of a hunting pack. But not all JRTs have this proper outlook, and the fact that many have been crossed with less amiable terriers in the quest for a JRT that could actually kill the fox (a fellow canid) has resulted in some JRTs that are not compatible with other dogs.

In most families, two JRTs of the opposite sex will get along just fine; however, a third JRT may not fit in so well. It is especially not advisable to leave more than two JRTs alone and unsupervised. If you have more than two JRTs, be warned that other dogs will often jump on and attack the loser in a scuffle. Neutered dogs are less likely to fight and neutering will prevent the headache of keeping Jack and Jill separated during her seasons. Nor are JRTs good with hamsters, gerbils, ferrets, and cats, unless raised with them or otherwise carefully trained and supervised.

Breeders have been extremely successful in producing a dog that fits the bill when it comes to bolting and dispatching foxes and small mammals, and the JRT is very likely the best hunting terrier in the world. If you want a hunting terrier, look no further—this is your breed. But if you want a quiet lapdog, keep on looking!

## Exercise Is Essential

This is not to say that the JRT cannot make a great pet—indeed, just the contrary! But they absolutely must have the chance to exercise both their body and mind with daily outdoor activity; otherwise, they are likely to exercise both by creating special effects on your home with their teeth and nails. Owners who want a JRT primarily as a pet must commit themselves to changing their lifestyles to fit that of the JRT, because compromise is not in this breed's vocabulary!

Although JRTs require an inordinate amount of exercise, they can derive as much joy from

*They keep going, and going, and going...*

killing toys in your living room as they could rats in the field. They will provide their owners with hours of entertainment with their robust sense of humor and clownish antics. They learn quickly, and are eager to please as long as fun is involved. JRTs are extremely loyal and fearless companions, and excellent watchdogs; a few can even be menacing protection dogs. They can make fun-loving friends for children, too, but they will not put up with any abusive treatment. They may not be the breed of choice for very young children who may not realize that they are being rough.

Of course JRTs sleep. But not very often.

# Health

Aside from the temperament traits needed to be a good hunting JRT, certain physical features are common to typical Jack Russell Terriers. The foremost is good health. Many popular pure breeds are plagued by hereditary health problems, but Jack Russell Terriers are affected by very few such problems. These include:

✔ Lens luxation, wherein the lens of one or (more commonly) both eyes becomes displaced, is the most prevalent hereditary disorder in the breed. Sometimes the detached lens will fall forward and even through the pupillary opening. Left untreated, the condition can result in secondary glaucoma and lead to loss of vision. This condition is believed to have a genetic basis, in part because it is more widespread in the terrier breeds than in any others; in fact, one researcher in England has reported seeing more cases in JRTs than in any other breed. This is not to imply that the breed is swamped with luxated lenses; however, it is a condition about which breeders and owners should be conscious.

✔ Primary glaucoma (increased pressure within the eye), corneal dystrophy (opacity of the clear surface of the eye), and progressive retinal atrophy (PRA, deterioration of the visual receptors of the retina) have also been reported in the breed, but are not believed to be widespread.

✔ Also reported is progressive neuronal abiotrophy (PNA, or ataxia), in which dogs develop tremors and severe lack of coordination, and ultimately are unable to stand or even eat. It results from the degeneration of cells in the cerebellum, that part of the brain responsible for making smooth, coordinated movements. The condition is believed to be hereditary, but again, is not widespread.

✔ Patellar luxation has been reported, but is now less common than in previous times. It is more common in shorter-legged JRTs. In this condition the patella (kneecap) slips from the groove in front of the knee and becomes displaced to the inside, rendering the dog unable to straighten the leg. Affected dogs may stand bowlegged or cow-hocked. Such dogs will hold the leg up for a few steps when moving until the patella pops back into place. The condition can be corrected surgically.

✔ Legg-Calvé-Perthes disease involves deterioration of the head of the femur (thigh bone), usually of one leg. It is usually not apparent until about seven months of age, when the dog may be slightly lame and tend to run on three legs. Degenerative joint disease eventually causes more severe lameness. Surgery may be necessary to prevent further damage.

✔ Deafness has been reported in one (unilateral) or both (bilateral) ears. Bilaterally deaf dogs should be apparent by the time the pups are of selling age, but it is difficult to detect a unilaterally deaf dog. A test (brain stem auditory evoked response, or BAER) is available at most veterinary teaching hospitals that can detect hearing loss in pups as young as five weeks of age by monitoring electrical impulses in the dog's brain in response to noises.

✔ Some JRTs have very short toes, so short that the nails appear to stick straight forward. The condition seems to be caused by premature closing of the growth plate. Although such toes would not be evident in a young pup, they seem to cause no problems and are of concern only if you want your JRT for competition or breeding.

✔ Also sometimes found in JRTs are missing teeth, occlusion problems, allergic dermatitis, and undescended testicles—problems common to all pure breeds.

Although any hereditary disease is one too many, the above list is short in the world of purebred dogs. The abundance of skeletal, retinal, and cardiac disorders common in so many other breeds have not made their appearance in Jack Russells. With responsible breeding, let's hope the list gets shorter, not longer.

The number one cause of death in Jack Russell Terriers is being hit by cars. Owner carelessness and blind trust are the insidious killers. Those that avoid accidents typically live to be 13 or 14 years of age, with unusual (but not rare) JRTs reaching 17 or 18 years.

# Conformation

Despite the fact that JRT breeders have traditionally not emphasized conformation, it does not mean that JRTs have been bred with no guidelines. Nothing could be further from the truth. But first and foremost, the guideline has been ability in the field.

Hunting JRTs must not only be willing to follow a fox (or other quarry) to ground, but they must be physically able to do so. This ability does require certain features of conformation, most notably strong legs, a flexible torso, and a small chest. The Parson Russell described the ideal JRT conformation as that "of an adult vixen red fox, approximately 14 inches (36 cm) at the withers and 14 pounds (6.4 kg) in weight."

JRTs should be able to do the job for which they were bred with a minimum of exertion and maximum of effect, and without becoming lame in the process. This attribute is known as *soundness*. Despite the emphasis upon function, breeders of JRTs also want their dogs to look like JRTs; that is, they should possess the attribute of the Jack Russell Terrier *type*. Add these attributes of soundness and type to the requirements of *good health* and *temperament,* and you have the four cornerstones of the ideal Jack Russell Terrier.

## Various Breed Standards

Several breed standards exist for the JRT. This, combined with the wide variety in size, coat, and type that is acceptable within the more popular of these standards, allows for great variation within the breed. This variability is one of the breed's attributes, allowing for specialization within the breed for hunting different quarry over different terrain. It is also the source of much disagreement, as some JRT purists believe the wide acceptance only promotes a generic terrier of questionable Jack Russell ancestry and type.

The original JRT standard was drafted in 1904 by the founder of the Parson Jack Russell Club, Arthur Heineman, and the current JRTAA standard was modeled after the Heineman standard.

*JRTs come in a variety of coat types.*

The JRTCA standard was drafted in 1975 and is also a popular standard by which the JRT is judged in America. Both standards describe the same tough and lively hunter, but with some subtle (and some important) differences.

# The JRTAA/AKC Standard of Perfection

## General Appearance

The Jack Russell Terrier was developed in the south of England in the 1800's as a white terrier to work European red fox both above and below ground. The terrier was named for the Reverend John Russell, whose terriers trailed hounds and bolted foxes from dens so the hunt could ride on.

To function as a working terrier, he must possess certain characteristics: a ready attitude, alert and confident; balance in height and length; medium in size and bone, suggesting strength and endurance. Important to breed type is a natural appearance: harsh, weatherproof coat with a compact construction and clean silhouette. The coat is broken or smooth. He has a small, flexible chest to enable him to pursue his quarry underground and sufficient length of leg to follow the hounds. Old scars and injuries, the result of honorable work or accident, should not be allowed to prejudice a terrier's chance in the show ring, unless they interfere with movement or utility for work or breeding.

## Size, Proportion, Substance

**Size:** Both sexes are properly balanced between 12 inches and 14 inches (30–36 cm) at the withers. The ideal height of a mature

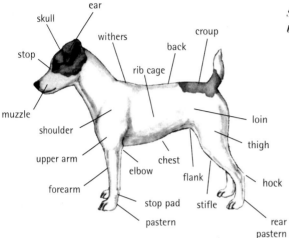

skull
ear
withers
stop
muzzle
rib cage
back
croup
shoulder
upper arm
elbow
forearm
chest
flank
stifle
stop pad
pastern
loin
thigh
hock
rear
pastern

*Some terms used in the Jack Russell Terrier breed standard.*

**Disqualification Height:** Under 12 inches or over 15 inches.

## Head

**Head:** Strong and in good proportion to the rest of the body, so the appearance of balance is maintained.

**Expression:** Keen, direct, full of life, and intelligence.

**Eyes:** Almond shaped, dark in color, moderate in size, not protruding. Dark rims are desirable.

**Ears:** Button ear. Small "V" shaped drop ears of moderate thickness carried forward close to the head with the tip so as to cover the orifice and pointing toward the eye. Fold is level with the top of the skull or slightly above. When alert, ear tips do not extend below the corner of the eye.

**Skull:** Flat and fairly broad between the ears, narrowing slightly to the eyes. The stop is well defined but not prominent.

**Muzzle:** Length from nose to stop is slightly shorter than the distance from stop to occiput.

**Jaws:** Upper and lower are of fair and punishing strength.

**Nose:** Must be black and fully pigmented.

**Bite:** Teeth are large with complete dentition in a perfect scissors bite, i.e., upper teeth closely overlapping the lower teeth and teeth set square to the jaws.

**Faults:** Light or yellow eye, round eye. Hound ear, fleshy ear, rounded tips.

**Disqualifications:** Prick ears. Liver color nose. Four or more missing teeth. Overshot, undershot, or wry mouth.

dog is 14 inches at the withers and bitches 13 inches (33 cm). Terriers whose heights measure either slightly larger or smaller than the ideal are not to be penalized in the show ring provided other points of their conformation, especially balance and chest span, are consistent with the breed standard. The weight of a terrier in hard working condition is usually between 13 to 17 lbs. (6–7.7 kg). Proportion balance is the keystone of the terrier's anatomy. The chief points of consideration are the relative proportions of skull and foreface, head and frame, height at withers and length of body. The height at withers is slightly greater than the distance from withers to tail, i.e. by possibly 1 to 1½ inches (2.5–3.8 cm) on a 14 inch (36 cm) dog. The measurement will vary according to height, the ratio of height to back being approximately 6:5.

**Substance:** The terrier is of medium bone, not so heavy as to appear coarse or so light as to appear racy. The conformation of the whole frame is indicative of strength and endurance.

## Neck, Topline, Body

**Neck:** Clean and muscular, moderately arched, of fair length, gradually widening so as to blend well into the shoulders.

**Topline:** Strong, straight, and level in motion, the loin slightly arched.

**Body:** In overall length to height proportion, the dog appears approximately square and balanced. The back is neither short nor long. The back gives no appearance of slackness but is laterally flexible, so that he may turn around in an earth. Tuck-up is moderate.

**Chest:** Narrow and of moderate depth, giving an athletic rather than heavily chested appearance; must be flexible and compressible.

*The JRTCA and AKC standards call for a dog that is approximately square, that is, about as long in body as it is tall in the withers.*

The ribs are fairly well sprung, oval rather than round, not extending past the level of the elbow.

**Tail:** Set high, strong, carried gaily but not over the back or curled. Docked so the tip is approximately level to the skull, providing a good handhold.

**Faults:** Chest not spannable or shallow; barrel ribs. Tail set low or carried over the back, i.e., squirrel tail.

## Forequarters

**Shoulders:** Long and sloping, well laid back, cleanly cut at the withers. Point of shoulder sits in a plane behind the point of the prosternum. The shoulder blade and upper arm are of approximately the same length; forelegs are placed well under the dog.

**Elbows:** Hang perpendicular to the body, working free of the sides. Legs are strong and

straight with good bone. Joints turn neither in nor out.

**Pasterns:** Firm and nearly straight.

**Feet:** Round, catlike, very compact, the pads thick and tough, the toes moderately arched pointing forward, turned neither in nor out.

**Fault:** Hare feet.

## Hindquarters

Strong and muscular, smoothly molded, with good angulation and bend of stifle. Hocks near the ground, parallel, and driving in action. Feet as in front.

## Coat

**Smooth:** Double-coated. Coarse and weatherproof. Flat but hard, dense, and abundant, belly and undersides of thighs are not bare.

**Broken:** Double-coated. Coarse and weatherproof. Short, dense undercoat covered with a

*Head and expression are integral to breed type, but can vary widely and still be correct.*

harsh, straight, tight jacket which lies flat and close to the body and legs. There is a clear outline with only a hint of eyebrows and beard. Belly and undersides of thighs are not bare. Coat does not show a strong tendency to curl or wave. No sculpted furnishings. The terrier is shown in his natural appearance not excessively groomed. Sculpturing is to be severely penalized.

**Faults:** Soft, silky, wooly, or curly topcoat. Lacking undercoat.

## Color

White, white with black or tan markings, or a combination of these, tricolor. Colors are clear. Markings are preferably confined to the head and root of tail. Heavy body markings are not desirable. Grizzle is acceptable and should not be confused with brindle.

**Disqualification:** Brindle markings.

## Gait

Movement or action is the crucial test of conformation. The terrier's movement is free, lively, well coordinated, with straight action in front and behind. There should be ample reach and drive with a good length of stride.

## Character and Temperament

Bold and friendly. Athletic and clever. At work, he is a game hunter, tenacious and courageous. At home, he is playful, exuberant, and overwhelmingly affectionate. He is an independent and energetic terrier and requires his due portion of attention. He should not be quarrelsome. Shyness should not be confused with submissiveness. Submissiveness is not a fault. Sparring is not acceptable.

**Fault:** Shyness.

**Disqualification:** Overt aggression towards another dog or human.

## Spanning

To measure a terrier's chest, span from behind, raising only the front feet from the ground, and compress gently. Directly behind the elbows is the smaller, firm part of the chest. The central part is usually larger but should feel rather elastic. Span with hands tightly behind the elbows on the forward portion of the chest. The chest must be easily spanned by average size hands. Thumbs should meet at the spine and fingers should meet under the chest. This is a significant factor and a critical part of the judging process. The dog can not be correctly judged without this procedure.

## Disqualifications

Height under 12 inches (30 cm) or over 15 inches (38 cm). Prick ears, liver nose. Four or more missing teeth. Overshot, undershot, or wry mouth. Brindle markings. Overt aggression towards other dogs or humans.

# The JRTCA Standard of Perfection

**Characteristics:** The terrier must present a lively, active, and alert appearance. It should impress with its fearless and happy disposition. It should be remembered that the Jack Russell is a working terrier and should retain these instincts. Nervousness, cowardice or overaggressiveness should be discouraged, and it should always appear confident.

**General Appearance:** A sturdy, tough terrier, very much on its toes all of the time, measuring between 10 inches and 15 inches (25–38 cm) at the withers. The body length must be in proportion to the height, and it should present a compact, balanced image, always being in solid, hard condition.

**Head:** Should be well-balanced and in proportion to the body. The skull should be flat, of moderate width at the ears, narrowing to the eyes. There should be a defined stop but not overly pronounced. The length of muzzle from the nose to the stop should be slightly shorter than the distance from the stop to the occiput. The nose should be black. The jaw should be powerful and well boned with strongly muscled cheeks.

**Eyes:** Should be almond shaped, dark in color, and full of life and intelligence.

**Ears:** Small V-shaped drop ears carried forward close to the head and of moderate thickness.

**Mouth:** Strong teeth with the top slightly overlapping the lower. (*Note:* A level bite is acceptable for registration.)

**Neck:** Clean and muscular, of good length, gradually widening at the shoulders.

**Forequarters:** The shoulders should be sloping and well laid back, fine at points, and clearly cut at the withers. Forelegs should be strong and straight-boned with joints in correct alignment. The elbows should be hanging perpendicular to the body and working free of the sides.

**Body:** The chest should be shallow and narrow, and the front legs set not too widely apart, giving an athletic, rather than heavily chested, appearance. As a guide only, the chest should be small enough to be easily spanned behind the shoulders, by average-size hands, when the terrier is in a fit, working, condition. The back should be strong, straight and, in comparison to the height of the terrier, give a balanced image. The loin should be slightly arched.

**Hindquarters:** Strong and muscular, well put together with good angulation and bend of stifle, giving plenty of drive and propulsion. Seen from behind, the hocks must be straight.

**Feet:** Round, hard-padded, of catlike appearance, neither turning in or out.

**Tail:** Should be set rather high, carried gaily and in proportion to body length, usually about 4 inches (10 cm) long, providing a good hand-hold.

**Coat:** Smooth, without being so sparse as to not provide a certain amount of protection from the elements and undergrowth. Rough or broken coated, without being wooly.

**Color:** White should predominate (i.e., must be more than 51 percent white) with tan, black, or brown markings. Brindle markings are unacceptable.

**Gait:** Movement should be free, lively, and well coordinated with straight action in front and behind.

**Special Notes:** Old scars or injuries, the result of work or accident, should not be allowed to prejudice a terrier's chance in the show ring unless they interfere with its movement or with its utility for work or stud.

A Jack Russell Terrier should not show any strong characteristics of another breed.

**Faults:**

✔ shyness
✔ disinterest
✔ overaggression
✔ defects in bite
✔ weak jaws
✔ fleshy ears
✔ down at the shoulder
✔ barrel ribs
✔ out at elbow
✔ narrow hips
✔ straight stifles
✔ weak feet
✔ sluggish or unsound movement
✔ dishing
✔ plaiting
✔ toeing
✔ silky or wooly coats
✔ too much color (less than 51 percent white)
✔ shrill or weak voice
✔ lack of muscle or skin tone
✔ lack of stamina or lung reserve
✔ evidence of foreign blood.

# Requirements for Registration with the JRTCA

Dogs applying for registration must be over one year of age and be owned by a member of

*The standard describes an athletic terrier that can keep up with a horse and fit into a small space.*

the JRTCA. Dogs failing in some requirements may not be registered, but can still be recorded, which enables them to compete in JRTCA hunting trials. However, JRTs under 10 inches (25 cm) or over 15 inches (38 cm) in height at the withers are ineligible for JRTCA registration or recording. Applications for registration must include:

✔ *Stud service certificate* signed by the owner of the dog's sire.

✔ *Four generation pedigree.* Products of inbreedings (mother/son, father/daughter, brother/sister) are not acceptable, and half sister/half brother matings are allowable only once in every three generations.

✔ *Official JRTCA veterinary certificate.* Dogs must be clear of defects of possible hereditary nature, such as cryptorchidism, eye problems, bite problems, luxated pattellas, and some hernias. A spay/neuter certificate will suffice in place of a veterinary certificate.

✔ *Color photographs.* Dogs must be evaluated from the front and both sides to ensure that they generally adhere to the breed standard. The photos must be signed by the veterinarian at the time the veterinary health certificate is signed.

# Requirements for Registration with the AKC

The AKC registers dogs according to evidence of pure breeding, which means that to receive full AKC registration both parents should be registered with the AKC or another registry recognized by the AKC. The JRTCA is not

among the AKC recognized registries. However, you can obtain an Indefinite Listing Privilege (ILP) registration number for a dog that looks sufficiently like a Jack Russell Terrier even though it may lack pedigree credentials, as long as the dog is spayed or neutered. An ILP number will enable your dog to compete in all AKC events for which JRTs are usually eligible except for conformation shows.

Unfortunately, under current circumstances, it is not possible to have dual (AKC and JRTCA) registered dogs or to compete at both JRTCA and AKC events. This schism results from an earnest disagreement about what is best for the breed's future; but all the dogs know is that they want to go have fun anywhere, whether it's AKC, JRTCA, or your backyard!

# FOR THE BEST

Your JRT-to-be should come from a reputable source that upholds the high standards with which this breed has come to be identified. Unfortunately, with increasing popularity, JRTs are found with greater frequency in backyard breeding pens. Don't encourage irresponsible breeding, and don't settle for less than the best this great breed has to offer. Your JRT will be a part of your family and life for the next 10 to 15 years. Spend the time now to make those years the best possible.

## Decisions, Decisions

### Puppy or Adult?

The easiest transition time for puppies is between 8 and 12 weeks of age, but if you definitely want a competition-quality dog you may have to wait until 5 or 6 months of age. No matter what the age, if the puppy has been properly socialized (that is, treated gently and exposed to a variety of situations, people, and dogs), your JRT will soon blend into your family life and love you as though he has always owned you.

Puppies are not for everyone, however. No one can deny that a puppy is cute and fun, but a young puppy is much like a baby; you can't ever be too busy to walk, feed, supervise, or clean (and clean and clean). Young JRT pups

*Is it puppy love?*

are actually fairly obedient but when they reach adolescence at around seven months of age, all rudiments of domestication may sometimes appear to be lost! If you work away from home, have limited patience, or heirloom rugs, an adult may be a better choice.

Most adult Jack Russells adjust quickly and can form new attachments in a short time. Still, older JRTs, especially kennel dogs, may have a difficult time adjusting to other pets or children. Obedience training is a necessity for both adolescents and adults if they are to live in a civilized world.

### Male or Female?

Both males and females have comparably wonderful and mischievous personalities. Many breeders believe the JRT males tend to be a little more people-oriented and sweeter, and the females a little busier and hunting motivated.

The bad points:

✔ Females come in estrus ("season" or "heat") twice a year; this lasts for three weeks, during which time you must keep her away from amorous neighborhood males who have chosen your house as the place to be. You must also contend with her bloody discharge and possible attempts to elope with her suitors.

✔ Males are apt to go off in search of females, and often think nothing of repeatedly lifting their leg on your furniture to mark your house as their territory.

The solution: **neutering.** Your JRT will be better behaved, cleaner, and possibly healthier if it is spayed or neutered at an early age.

✔ *Spaying* (surgical removal of ovaries and uterus) before the first season eliminates the estrous cycle and drastically reduces the chances of breast or uterine cancer.

✔ *Castration* (surgical removal of the testicles) eliminates the chance of testicular cancer. Dogs with undescended testicles have an increased risk of testicular cancer, and should be castrated before three to five years of age.

## Smooth, Rough, or In-between?

JRTs come in three coat types: smooth, rough, and broken.

✔ The broken coat is intermediate between the other types, having the appearance of a short coarse coat, perhaps with slight facial furnishings.

✔ The rough coat requires regular stripping (see page 75) if it is to keep its proper JRT neat appearance. All coat types shed year-round.

✔ Some JRT owners believe the smooth coat sheds more, but all hair sheds the same—the smooth hairs may just be better at weaving themselves into your clothing!

## JRTCA or AKC Registered?

Your JRT cannot be registered with both. The JRTCA is traditionally the registry of choice for

*Jack Russell Terriers come in many types, not all of which can compete in all competitions. Be sure you know the style of JRT that best fits your needs and taste.*

JRT owners, but AKC registration is growing and may surpass JRTCA in a short time. Both clubs offer a variety of activities. The AKC registers pups at birth, while the JRTCA will not register them until over a year of age. If you plan on breeding or in any way competing with your JRT, its registration body is a very important decision. Contact both clubs and see for yourself which ideals and activities you prefer.

## Short-legged or Long-legged?

The short-legged JRTs are very popular as pets, but are incorrect according to the AKC and JRTCA standards. In fact, some short-legged dogs have bowed front legs, the hallmark signature of an achondroplastic dwarf. Dwarf breeds exist in the dog world as a product of selective breeding, but the traditional Jack Russell Terrier is not one of them. Short-legged JRTs make wonderful pets, but don't expect to register them with the JRTCA or compete with them in AKC conformation (although disqualified dogs can compete in AKC performance events). If you want an AKC conformation or JRTCA competition-quality

*Bowed front legs are often seen on short-legged JRTs.*

dog, get a long-legged Jack Russell with a square, proportioned body.

Short-legged dogs have their own organization, the English Jack Russell Terrier Club of America. The EJRTCA standard calls for a dog 8 to 12 inches (21–31 cm) in height, slightly longer than tall, with legs as straight (unbowed) as is consistent with being short. The EJRTCA sponsors many competitive events of its own.

# All Dogs Are Not Created Equal

One of the reasons for choosing a purebred dog is the assurance that the dog will look and act a certain way when it matures. JRTs come in a wide range of types, but at some point an alleged JRT no longer even resembles a JRT. Why pay purebred prices for a dog that doesn't even resemble a pure breed?

## Registering Organization

In most breeds, the term "AKC registered" is touted as a major advertising point. In the JRT, JRTCA registration is at least as prestigious as AKC registration. In fact, because JRTCA registration is not automatically bestowed simply because the parents were registered, the JRTCA designation signifies that a dog not only is of pure parentage, but possesses certain minimal requirements of health and type.

*The short-legged, sometimes called "puddin," or English Jack Russell Terrier is a favorite with pet owners and is registered as a separate breed in many countries.*

Still, a key word here is *minimal.* If you want your JRT to be "just" a pet, then such minimal requirements are probably all that you will need. If, however, you want to compete with your JRT in terrier trials or other events, you will want to select a pup from parents that have themselves excelled in such endeavors.

No matter what your plans are for your new JRT, you should try to get a puppy from

parents that are both registered with either the AKC or JRTCA. You want to avoid a puppy from parents whose only claim to breeding quality is fertility, and you want to avoid buying from a breeder whose only claim to that title is owning a fertile dog. You may think that if you only want pet quality you don't have to be so careful, but consider the most important attributes of a pet: good health and good temperament.

Buy the best dog, with the best parents, from the best breeder possible. It is also best if you can see the parents and puppies in the flesh, and even better if you get some type of guarantee. But a word of caution about guarantees from any source: No guarantee can reimburse you for your broken heart when your puppy dies. And replacement guarantees that require you to return the original dog aren't worth much when you already love that original dog.

## How Dogs Are Graded

Dogs are generally graded as pet, show (or competition), and breeding quality, although these terms are less frequently used for JRTs.

✔ A pet-quality dog is one that has some cosmetic fault that would prevent it from winning in a conformation ring, terrier trial, or from receiving JRTCA registration. A pet should still be of good health and temperament. Being a pet is the most important role a dog can fulfill, and pet quality should never be scoffed at.

✔ Show- or competition-quality dogs should first of all be pet quality; that is, they should have good temperament and health. In addition, they should portray the attributes called for in the breed standard, and possess the potential to excel in the field.

✔ With few exceptions, breeding-quality dogs come from impeccable backgrounds, and are of even higher quality than are show/competition-quality dogs. Breeding quality means more than the ability to impregnate or conceive, but far too often these are the only criteria applied to prospective parents by owners unduly impressed by a registration certificate. It is difficult to pick a show-quality puppy at an early age; it is impossible to pick a breeding-quality puppy.

# Choose Your Source Carefully

The better quality you demand, the longer your search will take. A couple of months is a reasonable time to spend looking for a pet puppy, a couple of years for a breeding-quality

*Look to the parents for the dog your puppy will become.*

## TIP

### Breeder Danger Signals

✔ Breeders who use incorrect terms, such as thoroughbreds, full-blooded, spaded, or papered, or boast of a "long pedigree."

✔ Breeders of more than two different breeds of dogs. Most dedicated breeders spend years studying one breed and could never have the resources to do justice to several breeds. Multi-breed breeders are usually small scale puppy mills.

✔ Breeders of more than two or three litters per year, unless they are one of the top kennels in the country.

✔ Breeders who can't compare their dogs to the JRT standard, or don't know the standard.

✔ Breeders who do not BAER test their breeding stock.

✔ Breeders unfamiliar with any JRT health concerns.

✔ Breeders who insist you view the puppies at a place other than their home.

✔ Breeders who have no photos or videotapes of both parents and other relatives.

✔ Breeders who have no pedigree on hand.

✔ Breeders without registered stock.

✔ Breeders who do not allow you to visit the dam of a litter.

✔ Breeders who insist on "puppy-back" agreements, requiring you to breed your dog and give them puppies from the resulting litter.

✔ Breeders who ask you no questions.

✔ Breeders who think JRTs are ideal for everyone.

✔ Breeders who tell you that you can make your money back by breeding your JRT.

✔ Breeders who will not take the dog back at any time in its life should you not be able to keep it. Good breeders care about the welfare of the dog for its entire life, not just until it walks out the door.

✔ Cheap puppies. Expect to pay from $350 to $600 for a good quality JRT. Males and females should cost the same.

dog. Begin your search for a high-quality JRT by seeing as many JRTs as possible, talking to JRT breeders, attending JRT competitions, and reading every available JRT publication.

No matter what quality JRT you want, some sources are better than others. The best way to locate a JRT is to contact the JRTAA or JRTCA and ask for a list of breeders in your area, and for a schedule of coming events so that you can see a number of JRTs from different breeders in the flesh. *True Grit,* the JRTCA newsletter, is an excellent source for upcoming litter announcements. Another possibility is one of the all-breed dog magazines, such as *Dog World* (see Information, page 110).

### Breeders

Why contact a serious breeder if you "only" want a pet? Because these breeders will have raised your pet as though it were their next big winner. Your dog will have received the same prenatal care, nutrition, and socialization as every prospective competition dog in that litter. The pup has the benefit of the dedicated breeder's years of study of the breed. Such breeders should be knowledgeable and conscientious enough to have also considered temperament and health when planning the breeding. If this is to be your first Jack Russell Terrier, you will need continued advice from an experienced JRT owner as your puppy grows. The serious hobby breeder is just a phone call away, and will be concerned that both you and the puppy are getting along well. In fact, because many breeders will expect to keep in touch with the owners of all of the puppies throughout their lives, you may find yourself a member of an adopted extended family of sorts, all of whom are available for advice, help, consolation, and celebration.

## The Rescue JRT

There is one more alternative: the rescue JRT. You may find it doubly rewarding to provide a loving home for an adult JRT who has fallen upon hard times. Unfortunately, the JRTCA Russell Rescue commonly has more JRTs than homes. Most of these dogs simply had the misfortune of being owned by somebody who either could not cope with the typical JRT personality, or who bought a dog on a whim. The only thing worse for these dogs than not getting adopted is to be adopted by another unprepared or uncommitted family. Don't take your decision to get a rescue JRT any more lightly than your original decision to get a JRT. For the address of rescue groups, see page 108.

Much as you may be tempted to rush in and save one of these souls, take the time to first ascertain why that particular JRT did not work out for its former owner. If you are a new dog owner, it may be best to leave a dog with behav-ior problems for a more experienced owner to deal with. Speak with a veterinarian, knowledgeable dog trainer, or behaviorist and ask what the treatment and prognosis is for any behavior disorder. Most often, you will find that their only crime was being a typical JRT.

## Other Sources

Most dogs are not obtained through breed clubs, rescue organizations, or dog shows. Instead, they are usually obtained through friends, neighbors, newspaper ads, and pet shops.

The chances of your friend or neighbor being a knowledgeable JRT breeder are remote. Although there are exceptions, too many newspaper ads are placed by backyard breeders who typically know no more about breeding JRTs than to put a male and female together and see what comes out. A pet shop should be able to provide the same information about a puppy that you would get directly from the breeder: pedigrees, photos, and health records of the parents; whether the puppy was raised around loving people; how long it stayed with the mother; and so forth.

# Questions, Questions

Focus your attention on breeders who can boast of registered and titled stock, home-raised pups, and a willingness to discuss both pros and cons of the breed. A good breeder should ask you about your previous history with dogs, why you want a Jack Russell Terrier, what you know about living with one, and what living arrangements you have planned for the dog. Consider the following questions:

**1.** Ask about the parents. Are they AKC, JRTCA, (or if short-legged, EJRTCA) registered?

*Ask about all the particulars before visiting—and falling in love with—the puppies.*

If they are not JRTCA registered because they were of insufficient quality, then they should never have been allowed to produce puppies. If they are not registered because the breeder just didn't care to, this is another bad sign because it shows a careless attitude on the part of the breeder.

**2.** What kind of temperaments do the parents and the puppies have? Have the parents or puppies had any health problems? Have the parents been tested for any hereditary problems? If the breeder states that the parents have been tested for eye problems or deafness, then this is an excellent sign, even though breeders don't screen because problems are relatively rare. Ask questions such as, "Why did you breed the litter?" "How did you choose the sire?"

**3.** Ask about the terms of sale. Don't fall in love with a puppy and then have to walk away because an agreement could not be reached. There are several possibilities, the easiest being that you will pay a set amount (usually cash) and receive full ownership. Registration papers and pedigree should never cost extra. Sometimes breeders will insist upon having a pet puppy neutered before supplying the papers. If you are making installment payments, the breeder will probably retain the papers or a co-ownership until the last installment. Sometimes a breeder will insist upon co-owning the puppy permanently. If any co-ownership involves future breeding of the puppy (especially a female) and "puppy-back" agreements, you probably should shy away. If the co-ownership is for insurance that the dog will be returned to the breeder in the event you cannot keep it, such an

agreement is usually acceptable. Any such terms should be in writing.

Any time you buy a puppy, it should be done so with the stipulation that the purchase is pending a health check (at your expense) by your veterinarian. The breeder should furnish you with a complete medical history including dates of vaccinations and worming.

## Selecting a Puppy

Once you have narrowed down your list, if possible arrange to visit the breeder. Most modern "kennels" are a collection of only a few dogs that are first of all the breeder's pets. However large or small the operation, look for facilities

that are clean and safe. Again, these are clues about the care given your prospective puppy.

✔ Although it is virtually impossible to keep a litter of JRT puppies from creating an ongoing catastrophe, any messes should be obviously new. Old droppings are a sign of poor hygiene, and poor hygiene is a precursor to poor health.

✔ The adults should be clean, groomed, and in apparent good health. They should neither try to attack you nor cower from you.

✔ Look to the adults for the dog your puppy will become. If you don't care for their looks or temperaments, say good-bye. Do make allowances for the dam's ordeal of carrying and nursing, however. Ask to see a picture of her before breeding. If the sire is not on the premises, ask to see pictures of him as well. If such pictures are not available, the warning lights should go on. A reputable breeder will have so many pictures not only of the parents, but other dogs far removed in the pedigree, that you will wish you never asked!

*Choosing only one may just be impossible!*

✔ Always go to view the puppies prepared to leave without one if you don't see exactly what you want. Remember, no good breeder wants you to take a puppy you are not 110 percent crazy about. This is not something you can trade in once you find what you really want. Don't lead the breeder on if you have decided against a purchase; there may be another buyer in line.

## Picking the Healthiest JRT Pup

As you finally look upon this family of little busy-bodies, you may suddenly find it very difficult to be objective. How will you ever decide which one is best for you? If you want a show or working puppy, let the breeder decide. In fact, the breeder knows the puppies' personalities better than you will in the short time you can evaluate them, so listen carefully to any suggestions the breeder has, even for a pet. It is human nature to pick "extremes," but most breeders would advise against choosing either the boldest or quietest JRT puppy, or any pup that acts shy.

Several puppy aptitude tests have been popularized throughout the years. Most follow-up data have unfortunately indicated that they have little predictive value, so if you are determined to test the pups but your heart is still with a pup that didn't score on top, go with your heart. However, before doing any deciding between pups, first decide if this is the litter for you.

✔ By eight weeks of age, JRT pups should look like little Jack Russell Terriers.

✔ Dark nose pigmentation, absent at birth, should be present by this age.

✔ Feet and knuckles will be disproportionately large, but otherwise the pup should appear balanced, with front and rear legs approximately the same length.

✔ When viewed from the front or rear, the legs should be nearly parallel to each other, neither cow-hocked in the rear nor "east-west" or bow-legged in the front.

✔ Normal Jack Russell Terrier puppies are active, friendly, curious, and attentive. If they are apathetic or sleeping, it could be because they have just eaten, but it could also be because they are sickly.

✔ The puppies should be clean, with no missing hair, crusted or reddened skin, or signs of parasites. Eyes, ears, and nose should be free of discharge. Pups should not be coughing, sneezing, or vomiting.

✔ Examine the eyelids to ensure that the lids or lashes don't roll in on the eye.

*The chosen one.*

✔ The teeth should be straight and meet up evenly, with the top incisors just overlapping the bottom incisors.

✔ The gums should be pink; pale gums may indicate anemia.

✔ The area around the anus should have no hint of irritation or recent diarrhea.

✔ Pick up a fold of skin. It should "pop" back into place, adhering to the body. If it stays "tented" up, the pup could be dehydrated, which can result from repeated diarrhea or vomiting.

✔ Puppies should not be thin or potbellied. The belly should have no large bumps indicating an umbilical hernia.

✔ By the age of 12 weeks, male puppies should have both testicles descended in the scrotum.

If the puppy of your choice is limping, or exhibits any of the above symptoms, express your concern and ask to either come back the following week to see if it has improved, or to have your veterinarian examine it.

You may still find it nearly impossible to decide which little perpetual motion machine will be yours. Don't worry—no matter which one you choose, as long as it is from a good breeder and background, and you do your part to help it reach its potential, you will hit the jackpot of Jack Russells.

# LIFE WITH A JACK RUSSELL TERRIER

After finally finding your JRT pup, it's only natural to want to bring him home right away. But take a minute to look around your house. Is it really ready to withstand a juvenile Jack attack? It will be a lot easier to get it into terrier-proof shape now than it will be when you have a little puppy underfoot undoing everything just as fast as you can do it! So channel your excitement and make sure everything is just perfect and waiting for the new addition.

If you are contemplating bringing your pup home as a Christmas present, think again! The heartwarming scene you may have imagined of the children discovering the puppy asleep among the other gifts beneath the tree on Christmas morning is not realistic. The real scene is more often that of a crying, confused puppy who may have vented his anxiety on the other gifts and left you some additional "gifts" of his own beneath the tree! Don't bring a new puppy into the hectic chaos of Christmas morning. Not only does this add to what is bound to be a very confusing and intimidating transition for your JRT, but a puppy should not be expected to compete with all of the toys and games that children may be receiving. Every pup needs the undivided attention of his new family at this crucial time in his life. Instead, a photograph or videotape of your special Jack

*Home sweet home is made all the sweeter—and a lot more exciting— with a Jack Russell Terrier.*

Russell-to-be, or a stocking of puppy paraphernalia, should provide sufficient surprise, and give the whole family time to prepare.

## Keeping One Step Ahead

The number one JRT safety item is a securely fenced yard. Jack Russell Terriers are notorious ramblers. In today's world of automobiles and suburbs, a loose dog is at best an unwelcome visitor and, more often, a dead dog. JRTs are gifted jumpers, climbers, burrowers, and squeezers. They will find the smallest vulnerable spot in any fence.

The JRT's gift for digging can enable it to tunnel to freedom with uncanny speed. Not only should the bottom of your fence extend well underground, but you should also lay wire on, or just under, the ground extending for a few feet inside the yard. This prevents the dog from digging directly down next to the fence.

Many dogs are actually inadvertently taught to escape by their owners. Perhaps the new owner has an old fence, and decides to wait and see if it will hold the dog. When the dog squeezes out of the weakest spots, the owner patches those. But now the dog has learned that the fence is not impenetrable, and seeks out another, less obvious weak spot. Finally the dog is creating his own weak spots, jumping Olympic heights, burrowing to China, and squeezing through holes that you would swear couldn't possibly accommodate a dog with bones—and its owner taught him to do it. If you wanted your JRT to learn to squeeze through small passages or jump great heights, wouldn't you do so a little at a time? Then why use the same tactic to teach your dog *not* to squeeze through? If you want your dog to stay in the yard, make the yard Jack Russell Terrier-proof from the very beginning.

Your fence must not only be strong enough to keep your dog in, but to keep stray dogs out. This is why the "invisible fences" that keep your dog in the yard are less than optimal. They only work with a dog wearing a special shock collar that is activated by the buried boundary wire. They can't keep out stray dogs that aren't wearing such a collar. In addition, an excited or particularly strong-willed dog—such as a Jack Russell—can just "grit its teeth" and charge right through the boundary.

## Dangers in the Yard

There can still be dangers within the yard. If you leave your JRT alone in your yard, lock your gate, and take precautions to not make

your defenseless friend a target for Russell rustlers. Check for poisonous plants, bushes with sharp, broken branches at JRT eye level, and trees with dead branches or heavy fruits in danger of falling. If you have a pool, be aware that, although dogs are natural swimmers, a little JRT cannot pull himself up a swimming pool wall, and he could drown. Plug up any holes leading under the house that might lead a terrier into temptation.

## Dangers Inside

Terrier-proofing your home has two goals: protecting your dog, and protecting your home. The first step is to do everything you would do to baby-proof your home. Get down at puppy level and see what dangers beckon.
✔ Puppies love to chew electrical cords in half, and even lick outlets. This can result in death from shock, severe burns, or loss of jaw and tongue tissue.
✔ Jumping up on an unstable object (such as a bookcase) could cause it to come crashing down, perhaps crushing the puppy.
✔ Do not allow the puppy near the edges of high decks, balconies, or staircases. Use temporary plastic fencing or chicken wire in dangerous areas.
✔ Doors can be a hidden danger area. Everyone in your family must be made to understand the danger of slamming a door, which could catch a small dog and break a leg—or worse. Use doorstops to ensure that the wind does not suddenly blow doors shut, or that the puppy does not go behind the door to play. This can be a

*Don't bring a new puppy home at Christmas; it's best to get your dog well before or after the hectic holidays.*

danger, because the gap on the hinged side of the door can catch and break a little leg if the door is closed. Be especially cautious with swinging doors; a puppy may try to push one open, become caught, try to back out, and strangle. Clear glass doors may not be seen, and the puppy could be injured running into them. *Never* close a garage door with a JRT running about. Finally, doors leading to unfenced outdoor areas should be kept securely shut. A screen door is a vital safety feature; Jack Russells are adept at streaking between your legs to freedom when you open the front door.

## Household Furnishings and Personal Belongings

A JRT pup left alone can be an accomplished one-dog demolition team. Leather furniture is the world's biggest rawhide chewy to a puppy, and wicker can provide hours of chewing enjoyment (and danger to the dog from splintering). Anything with fur is definite terrier bait. Puppies particularly like to chew items that carry your scent. Shoes, eyeglasses, and clothing must be kept out of the youngster's reach. Remove anything breakable that you value from your JRT's reach. Remove books and papers. No need for a costly paper shredder when you have a puppy! Move any houseplants that you would like to survive. The ingenuity of the Jack Russell Terrier is never so obvious as when one is looking for trouble.

Your carpets (at least in the area between the cage and the door) can be covered with small washable rugs or indoor/outdoor carpeting until your puppy is housebroken. If you use an X-pen (see page 39), cover the floor beneath it with thick plastic (an old shower curtain works well), and then add towels or washable rugs for traction and absorbancy.

═══════ **T I P** ═══════

### Household JRT Killers

The following are potentially lethal to your inquisitive pet:
✔ rodent, snail, and insect baits
✔ antifreeze
✔ household cleaners
✔ toilet fresheners
✔ drugs
✔ chocolate (especially baker's chocolate)
✔ nuts, bolts, pennies
✔ pins and needles, and, in fact, anything in a sewing basket
✔ chicken bones or any bone that could be swallowed.

## Jack Tack

When it comes to accessories for your JRT, it's not really true that "all you add is love" (but you'll need lots of that, too)! The best sources for equipment are large pet stores, dog shows, and discount pet catalogs. Your welcome basket should include:
✔ **buckle collar**—to wear around the house.
✔ **choke collar or harness**—safer for walking on lead.
✔ **leash**—nylon, web, or leather—never chain! An adjustable show lead is good for puppies.
✔ **lightweight retractable leash**—better for older adult; be sure not to drop the leash as it may retract toward the pup and frighten him.
✔ **stainless steel flat-bottomed food and water bowls**—avoid plastic; it can cause allergic reactions and hold germs.

✔ **cage**—just large enough for an adult dog to stand up in without having to lower his head.

✔ **exercise pen**—tall enough that an adult dog can't jump over, or preferably with a top.

✔ **toys**—latex squeakies, fleece type toys, ball, stuffed animals, stuffed socks. Make sure the toys have no parts, such as squeakers or plastic eyes, that can be pulled off and swallowed.

✔ **chewbones**—the equivalent of a teething ring for babies.

✔ **anti-chew preparations,** such as Bitter Apple. The unpleasant taste discourages pups from chewing on items sprayed with it.

✔ **baby gate(s)**—better than a shut door for placing parts of your home off-limits.

✔ **brush and comb**

✔ **nail clippers**

✔ **poop scoop**—two-piece rake-type is best for grass.

✔ **dog shampoo** (see page 76 for choices)

✔ **first aid kit** (see page 89 for contents)

*Every waking moment means playtime for a JRT youngster; by supplying plenty of toys you can avoid your precious belongings being turned into JRT rubbish.*

✔ **sweater**—for cold climates.

✔ **food**—start with the same food the pup is currently eating.

✔ **dog bed**—a round fleece-lined cat bed is perfect, but you can also use the bottom of a plastic cage, or any cozy box with padding. Wicker will most likely be chewed to shreds.

✔ **camera and film!** (Telephoto lens is a big help.)

## The Den

A cage (or crate) is the canine equivalent of an infant's crib. It is a place for naptime, a place where you can leave your pup without worry that he will hurt himself or your home. It is not a place for punishment, nor is it a storage box for your dog when you're through playing. Place the cage in a corner of a quiet room, but not too far from the rest of the family. Place the pup in the cage when he begins to fall asleep, and he will become accustomed to using it as his bed. Be sure to place a soft blanket in the bottom. Also, by taking the pup directly from the cage to the outdoors upon awakening, the cage will be one of the handiest house-breaking aids at your disposal.

Many new dog owners are initially appalled at the idea of putting their pet in a cage as though it were some wild beast. At times, though, any puppy can seem like a wild beast, and a cage is one way to save your home from ruination and yourself from insanity. A cage can also provide a quiet haven for your youngster. Just as you hopefully find peace and security as you sink into your own bed at night, your pup needs a place that he can call his own, a place he can seek out whenever the need for rest and solitude arises. Used properly, your JRT will come to think of his cage not as a way to keep himself in, but as a way to keep others out!

## The X-Pen

An exercise pen (or "X-pen") fulfills many of the same functions as a cage. X-pens are transportable wire folding "playpens" for dogs, typically about 4 feet by 4 feet (1.2 m). X-pens are the perfect solution when you must be gone for a long time, because the pup can relieve

*Every dog should have a bed he can call his own.*

himself on paper in one corner, sleep on a soft bed in the other, and frolic with his toys all over! It's like having a little yard inside. Sometimes even the most devoted owners need a break from the constant antics of their JRT. The X-pen provides a safe time-out area when you just need some quiet time for yourself. But before leaving your pup in an X-pen, make sure that he cannot jump or climb out. Covers are available for incorrigible escapees.

## The Run of the House

Don't let your JRT puppy have the run of the entire house. Choose an easily puppy-proofed room where you spend a lot of time, preferably one that is close to a door leading outside. Kitchens and dens are usually ideal. When you must leave your dog for some time, you may wish to place him in a cage, X-pen, secure room, or outdoor kennel. Bathrooms have the disadvantage of being so confining and isolated that puppies may become destructive; garages have the disadvantage of also housing many poisonous items. Don't get a JRT and banish him to the far corners of the yard. Although your dog can spend a good part of his time outdoors in nice weather, why get a dog at all if you don't plan on welcoming him as a real member of your family? Your JRT will want to be in the thick of things, and participate in everything your family does.

So plan for your dog to be quartered in the house where he can be around activity, but not necessarily always underfoot. If you plan on leaving your dog in the yard for extended periods, you must provide a snug doghouse.

## The Scoop

The least glamorous, yet essential, item on your list is the poop scoop. What goes in must come out, and hopefully in your yard. Many dog owners never step foot in their own backyards because of dog excrement. Dogs raised in unclean yards grow used to stepping in feces and will continue to do so with reckless abandon their entire lives, an especially disgusting

trait if your dog sleeps in your bed or tends to jump up on you. Start early and keep your yard meticulously scooped, except for a sample pile in the area you wish the dog to continue using as his toilet area. Don't make your JRT live in a minefield.

# Creating a Civilized Housedog

Your new pup faces the transition from canine litter member to human family member. Every day will be full of novel experiences and new rules. Your pup is naturally inquisitive and will need you to guide him toward becoming a well-mannered member of the household.

### Off-Limits Training

You should have decided before your puppy came home what parts of your home will be off limits. Make sure that every family member understands the rules, and that they understand that sneaking the puppy onto off-limits furniture, for example, is not doing the puppy any favor at all. Your puppy will naturally want to explore every nook and cranny of your house. Part of the pup's exploratory tools are his teeth, and any chewed items left in his wake are your fault, not your pup's—you are the one who should have known better. Harsh corrections are no more effective than a tap on the nose along with a firm *"No,"* and removal of the item.

JRTs love to be up on furniture and other high places, but if you don't want to allow such behavior, start early. A harsh *"No!"* and firm but gentle push away from the furniture should let him realize that this is neither acceptable nor

*Do fence me in!*

*The X-pen is a safe yard within the home.*

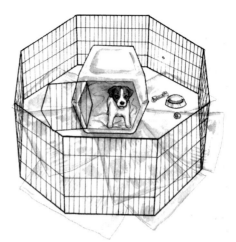

rewarding behavior. Don't fling the pup off the furniture, or use mousetraps on furniture surfaces; both practices are dangerous and a terrible idea unless you like emergency visits to the vet. There are several more humane items (available through pet catalogs) that emit a loud tone when a dog jumps on furniture, but these should not be necessary if you train your young puppy gently and consistently from the beginning.

## Housebreaking

Housebreaking is easier—and more difficult—than you might think. Most people have unrealistic expectations of their dog's ability to become housebroken, based in part upon friends' boasting about their little genius that was housebroken at two weeks of age or something similarly ludicrous. No matter how wonderful and smart your Jack is, he probably will not have full control over his elimination until he's around six months of age, and may not be reliably housebroken until a year old. Avoiding these common mistakes can hasten the process:

**Housebreaking blunder #1:** The number one housebreaking mistake made by most puppy owners is to give their puppies too much unsupervised freedom in the house. All canines have a natural desire to avoid soiling their denning area. The den area is considerably smaller than your entire house, however, and it will take some training before your pup extends the notion of den to your home.

You can use your dog's cage as his den, but if the cage is too large, the puppy may simply step away from the area he sleeps in and relieve himself at the other end of the cage. An overly large cage can be divided with a secure barrier

until the puppy is larger or housebroken. Even so, your puppy may step just outside the door of the cage and eliminate there, because to the pup, that fulfills the natural requirement of not going in the den. The puppy has failed to realize that he has just soiled *your* den. And the more the pup soils in a particular spot, the more he is likely to return to that same spot.

**Housebreaking blunder #2:** The second big mistake puppy owners make is to allow accidents to happen. Puppies have very weak control over their bowels, so if you don't take them to their elimination area often, they may not be able to avoid soiling. Puppies, like babies, have to eliminate a lot. You can't just stick them in a cage all day while you are at work and think you won't return home to a messy cage and messy pup. A rule of thumb is that a puppy can, at most, hold his bowels for as many hours as the pup is months old. This means that a three-month-old can hold himself for three hours. If the pup is forced to stay in a cage longer, you are setting the stage for a big problem. Once he gets used to eliminating in his cage, he may continue.

Puppies tend to relieve themselves in areas that smell like urine. This is why it is so critical to never let the pup have an accident indoors; if he does, clean and deodorize the spot thoroughly and block the pup's access to that area. Use a pet deodorizer cleaner, and never use one containing ammonia. Ammonia is a component of urine, so using an ammonia cleaner is like posting a sign that says "go here!"

If you cannot be with your puppy for an extended period, you may wish to leave him outside (only in good weather and with cover) so that he won't be forced to have an indoor accident. If this is not possible, you may have to paper train your puppy. Place newspapers on the far side of the room (or X-pen), away from the puppy's bed or water bowl; near a door to the outside is best. Place the puppy on the papers as soon as he starts to relieve himself.

A better option is to use sod squares instead of newspapers. Place the sod on a plastic sheet and, when soiled, take it outside and hose it off or replace it. By using sod, you are training the pup to relieve himself on the same surface he should eventually use outside. Place the soiled squares outside in the area you want your dog to use.

Because dogs are creatures of habit, housebreaking is more a matter of prevention than correction. To avoid accidents, learn to predict when your puppy will have to relieve himself. Immediately after awakening, and soon after heavy drinking or playing, your puppy will urinate. You will probably have to carry a younger baby outside to get him to the toilet area on time. Right after eating, or if nervous, your puppy will have to defecate. Circling, whining, sniffing, and generally acting worried usually signals that defecation is imminent. Even if the puppy starts to relieve himself, quickly but calmly scoop the pup up and carry him outside (the surprise of being picked up will usually cause the puppy to stop in midstream, so to speak). You can also clap your hands or make a loud noise to startle the pup so that he stops. You can add a firm "No," but yelling and swatting are actually detrimental. When the puppy does relieve himself in his outside toilet, remember to heap on the praise and let your pup know how pleased you are. Adding a food treat really gets the point across. Keep some in a jar near the door and always accompany your pup outside so that you can reward him.

**Housebreaking blunder #3:** The number three housebreaking mistake made by dog owners is overuse of punishment. Even if you catch your dog in the act, overly enthusiastic correction tends only to teach the dog not to relieve himself in your presence, even when outside. This is why you should reward with a tidbit when the pup does relieve himself outside. Punishment doesn't make clear what is desired behavior, but reward makes it clear very quickly. Punishing a dog for a mess he has made earlier is totally fruitless; it only succeeds in convincing the dog that every once in a while, for no apparent reason, you are apt to go insane and attack him. It is a perfect recipe for ruining a trusting relationship. That "guilty" look you may think your dog is exhibiting is really fear that you have once again lost your mind.

**Housebreaking blunder #4:** The number four housebreaking mistake owners make is to open the door and push the pup outside by himself. After five minutes, the pup is let back in and promptly relieves himself on the rug. Bad dog? No, bad owner. Chances are the pup spent his time outside trying to get back inside to his owner. Puppies do not like to be alone, and

*JRT pups are part beaver—keep them away from furniture!*

knowing you are on the other side of the door makes the outdoors unappealing. In bad weather, the pup probably huddled against the door so he didn't miss it when it was again opened. The solution? You must go outside with the pup every time. Don't take him for a walk, don't play with him, simply go with him to his relief area, say "*Hurry up*" (the most popular choice of command words), and be ready to praise and perhaps give a treat when the pup does his deed. Then you can go to his play area or back inside.

As soon as you are convinced your precocious puppy is housebroken, don't be surprised if he takes a giant step backward and convinces you there is no link between his brain and bowels. Keep up the good work, and things really will get better!

# Jack Russell Terrors

Terriers are known mischief makers, and Jack Russell Terriers are no exception. Indeed, this is one of the most endearing traits of the breed. But often misbehavior causes problems for their family or themselves, sometimes creating an intolerable situation. Despairing owners blame the dog, yet most of these problems can be avoided or cured.

Misuse of punishment is a major cause of continuing problems. If punishment doesn't work the first time, why do owners think that it will work the second, third, or fourth time?

## Hyperactivity

Most dogs labeled hyperactive by their owners are really not, but just underexercised normal dogs for their breed. The JRT is an active breed and you need to find ways to channel your dog's

*Jack Russells have loud barks—the better to be heard when they are underground, but a nuisance to your neighbors when they are above ground!*

over. Of course, you can't expect your JRT to know the difference. Instead, teach your dog to sit and stay, and then be sure to kneel down to his level for greetings. When your JRT does jump up, simply say *"No"* and step backward, so that his paws meet only air. Teaching your dog a special command that lets him know it's OK to jump up (when you're in your bum clothes) can actually help him determine the difference.

Shutting your dog in another room when guests arrive will only make him more crazed to greet people and ultimately worsen the problem. The more people he gets a chance to greet politely, the less excited he will be about meeting new people, and the less inclined he will be to jump up. Have your guests kneel and greet your sitting JRT.

energy. Set times for walks, games, and obedience. Although your dog will slow down with age, this is years in the future. In severe cases you may wish to consult with your dog's breeder, other JRT owners, Russell Rescue (see page 108), a behaviorist, or your veterinarian. If they agree your dog is simply a normal JRT (and he probably is), you can either wait for age to slow him down, or find him a home with someone already familiar and happy with Jack Russell high spirits.

## Jumping Up

Puppies naturally greet their mother and other adult dogs by licking them around the corners of their mouth. This behavior translates to humans, but in order to reach your face they need to jump up on you. Sometimes owners love this display of affection, but not when they are all dressed up or when company comes

## Barking

Having a doggy doorbell can be handy, but there is a difference between a dog that will warn you of a suspicious stranger and one that will warn you of the presence of oxygen in the air. The surest way to make your neighbors dislike your dog is to let him create a racket. Allow your JRT to bark momentarily at strangers, and then call him to you and praise him for quiet behavior, distracting him with an obedience exercise if need be.

Isolated dogs will often bark as a means of getting attention and alleviating loneliness. Even if the attention gained includes punishment, the dog will continue to bark in order to obtain the temporary presence of the owner.

The simplest solution is to move the dog's quarters to a less isolated location. For example, if barking occurs when your pup is put to bed, move his bed into your bedroom. If this is not possible, the pup's quiet behavior must be rewarded by the owner's presence, working up to gradually longer and longer periods. The distraction of a special chew toy, given only at bedtime, may help alleviate barking. The pup that must spend the day home alone is a greater challenge. Again, the simplest solution is to change the situation, perhaps by adding another animal—a good excuse to get two JRTs!

**But warning:** Some Jack Russells also like to bark when playing!

Ultrasonic collars emit an irritating sound every time your dog barks, and can often persuade a dog to stop barking. Anti-bark shock collars give the dog a mild electrical shock with each bark, and can be even more effective. Citronella collars squirt out a whiff of an irritating scent whenever the dog barks, and are usually more effective than shock collars. In all cases, you must be careful that the collars do not respond to other dogs barking!

## Digging

JRTs are naturally interested in what may lay beneath the earth (after all, the word "terrier" is derived from "terra," denoting these dogs' inclination to go to ground). Don't get a JRT if you can't stand the sight of holes. The only cure for digging is a lot of exercise and a lot of supervision, and fencing off those parts of the yard that you absolutely can't tolerate being turned into a moonscape. Remedies based on harsh corrections are not successful.

*Digging is first nature to a JRT.*

## Car Chasing

Keep the dog in the yard! JRTs have a weakness for rolling wheels. If you must try to effect a cure, either stop the car as soon as chasing begins, or carry along a high-tech long-distance squirt gun and spray the dog from the car. Of course, most JRTs will think that's just part of the grand game, too!

## Home Destruction

Many a Jack Russell owner has returned home to a disaster area and suspected that Jack the Ripper must have broken in the house. JRTs may be small, but they can be talented home redecorators.

Puppies are natural demolition dogs, and the best cure is adulthood, although adult dogs still may dig or destroy items through frustration or boredom. The best way to deal with

these dogs is to tire them out with both physical interaction (such as chasing a ball) and mental interaction (such as practicing a few simple obedience commands) on a daily basis.

More commonly, destructive behavior in an adult dog is due to separation anxiety. Dogs are highly social animals, and being left alone is an extremely stressful condition for many of them. They react by becoming agitated and trying to escape from confinement and, in fact, most of their destructive behavior is focused around doors and windows. Most owners believe their dog is "spiting" them for leaving, and they then punish the dog. Unfortunately, punishment is ineffective, because it actually increases the anxiety level of the dog, as he comes to both look forward to and dread his owner's return.

**The proper therapy** is treatment of the dog's fear of being left alone. This is done by leaving the dog alone for very short periods of time and gradually working to longer periods, taking care to never allow the dog to become anxious during any session. When you must leave the dog for long periods during the conditioning program, leave him in a different part of the house than the one in which the conditioning sessions take place, so that you don't undo all your work by letting the dog become overstressed by your long absence.

In either case, when you return home, no matter what the condition of the house or apartment, greet the dog calmly or even ignore him for a few minutes, to emphasize the point that being left was really no big deal. Then have the dog perform a simple trick or obedience exercise so that you have an excuse to praise him. It takes a lot of patience, and often a whole lot of self-control, but it's not fair to you or your dog to let this situation continue.

## Fearfulness

Despite their generally fearless attitude, JRTs can develop phobias and other fears. Never push your dog into situations that might overwhelm him. Never force a dog that is afraid of strangers to be petted by someone he doesn't know; it in no way helps the dog overcome his fear and is a good way for the stranger to get bitten. Strangers should be asked to ignore shy dogs, even when approached by the dog. Dogs seem to fear the attention of a stranger more than they fear the strangers themselves. When the dog gets braver, have the stranger offer him a tidbit, at first while not even looking at the dog. A program of gradual desensitization, with the dog exposed to the frightening person or thing and then rewarded for calm behavior, is time consuming but the best way to alleviate any fear.

Never coddle your dog when he acts afraid, because it reinforces the behavior. It is always useful if your JRT knows a few simple commands (see HOW-TO: Basic Training, page 66); performing these exercises correctly gives you a reason to praise the dog and also increases the dog's sense of security because he knows what is expected of him. Whether it is a fear of strangers, dogs, car rides, thunder, or being left alone, the concept is the same—never hurry, and never push the dog to the point that he is afraid.

## Aggression

The best cure for aggression is prevention, and the best prevention is to obtain your pup from a reputable breeder and to raise him with kindness, gentleness, and firmness, never encouraging biting or displays of dominance, and never punishing for deeds the dog cannot comprehend. Expose the pup to kind strangers from a young age, and make these interactions pleasurable.

*JRTs hate being left home alone.*

**Is it really aggression?** Puppies and dogs play by growling and biting. Usually, they play with their littermates this way, but if yours is an only puppy, you will just have to do. So many people have seen horror stories about dogs that when their pup growls and bites they immediately label him as a problem biter. You need to know the difference between true aggression and playful aggression. Look for these clues that tell you it's all in good fun:

✔ wagging tail
✔ down on elbows in front, with the rump in the air (the play-bow)
✔ barks intermingled with growls
✔ lying down or rolling over
✔ bounding leaps or running in circles
✔ mouthing or chewing on you or other objects

On the other hand, look for these clues to know you better watch out:

✔ low growl combined with a direct stare
✔ tail held stiffly
✔ sudden, unpredictable bites
✔ growling or biting in defense of food, toys, or bed
✔ growling or biting in response to punishment.

Chances are your JRT is simply playing. Still, this doesn't mean you should let him use you as a chewstick. When your pup bites you simply say "*Ouch! No!*" and replace your body part with a toy. Hitting your dog is uncalled for— your dog was just trying to play and meant no harm. Hitting also is a form of aggression that could give your dog the idea that he had better try (bite) harder next time because you're playing the game a lot rougher.

**Aggression toward other dogs:** Aggression toward other animals does not mean a dog will

be aggressive toward people. It's natural for your dog to defend his territory against strange dogs. The problem develops when your dog thinks the world is his personal territory. Many JRTs just don't see eye-to-eye with their fellow dogs.

Problems between housemates are most likely to occur between dogs of the same sex and age. Seniority counts for a lot in the dog world, and a young pup will usually grow up respecting his elders. Sometimes, however, a youngster gets aspirations to be top dog, or two dogs of about the same age never quite decided which one was leadership material. Then the trouble starts. Remember to first decide if this is natural rough play behavior between the two. An occasional disagreement is normal too. A disagreement that draws blood or leaves one dog screaming or in which the two dogs cannot be separated is a potential problem. Repeated disagreements spell trouble. Neutering one or both males in a two-male dominance battle can sometimes help, but neutering females will not.

It's human nature to soothe the underdog and punish the bully, but you'd be doing the underdog the worst favor you could. If your dogs are fighting for dominance, they are doing so in part because in the dog world, the dominant dog gets the lion's share of the most precious resources—which means your attention! If you give your attention to the loser, the winner will only try harder to beat the daylights out of the loser so your attention will go where it should go—to the winner. You will do your losing dog the best favor if you treat the winning dog like a king, and the losing dog like a prince. This means you always greet, pet, and feed the top dog first. It goes against human nature, but it goes with dog nature.

**Aggression toward humans:** Much has been made of dominance problems in dogs; they probably occur less often than is thought, but when they do occur, the results can be aggression toward family members. Aggression toward humans is uncommon in JRTs; when it does happen, the best advice is to seek advice from a dog behaviorist. Remember, dominance aggression does not refer to the occasional nip in play or even disobedience. It is a serious situation in which the dog actively challenges and bites, or threatens to bite, a member of the family. Because it is a serious situation, it calls for serious treatment that is uncalled for in other cases.

**Stopping a dogfight:** If a fight is about to break out, try to distract the dogs (perhaps with the promise of a walk) or spray them with water. Yelling or grabbing tends to escalate the tension and increase the chances of a fight. If a fight ensues, douse the combatants with water, or throw blankets over each of them. Fighting dogs have bad aim, so keep away from those teeth! If two people are present, as a last resort, grab the dogs by their hind legs and pull them off the ground, holding the dog away from your body. Some people keep a tub of water handy and actually throw the fighters

*Tug games are fine for most dogs, but not for aggressive ones. Teach your dog a release word that lets him understand you call the shots. Do this by saying "Give" and exchanging a treat for the toy.*

in it in order to separate them. Of course, if the dogs aren't next to the tub at the time, it is of little help. Others keep a cattle prod on hand with which to break up fighters. The cattle prod gives the dog a shock, which may or may not distract the dog enough to stop fighting. Unfortunately, it can also goad some dogs on to more vigorous fighting. Sometimes dragging the dogs to a doorway and closing the door between them can help.

**Introducing new dogs:** When introducing new dogs, it is best if both are taken to a neutral site so that territoriality does not provoke aggression. Two people walking the dogs beside each other as they would on a regular walk is an ideal way for dogs to accept each other. However, some JRTs are more aggressive when on lead, so make sure there is something to interest both dogs besides each other. If you are still worried, muzzle both dogs before letting them loose together.

## Other Animals

JRTs can be trustworthy around farm stock and household pets, including cats, but don't tempt them with hamsters and rats. Introduce your JRT to your cat gradually, inside the house. The dog should be held on leash initially, and the cat prevented from running, which would elicit a chase response in the dog. If the dog is fed every time the cat appears, he will come to appreciate the cat's presence. Don't leave them unsupervised unless you are absolutely sure of your JRT's good intentions.

## Introducing New People

Dogs that are tied up just out of reach of activity are prime candidates to be biters. Dogs that are hustled out of the room when guests arrive, or out of the family activities when a new baby arrives, will sometimes bite out of resentment. Teach your JRT to look forward to guests and children by rewarding proper behavior, such as sitting and staying in their presence, and by having them offer the dog a treat. A drastic measure is to withhold attention from the dog except in the presence of guests or the baby, so that the dog associates being with them as something that brings attention and rewards.

Of course, it should hardly be mentioned that no baby or child should be allowed to play roughly with or tease your JRT; one could hardly blame a small dog that growls or bites out of self-defense, but one could blame an owner for letting the situation develop.

Unlike in humans, where direct eye contact is seen as a sign of sincerity, staring a dog directly in the eye is interpreted by the dog as a threat. It can cause a fearful dog to bite out of what he perceives as self-defense, and is responsible for many dog bites.

## Dominance Aggression

Dominance aggression most often occurs as a result of competition over a resource (such as trying to remove food or a toy, encroaching on his sleeping quarters, or trying to step past him in a narrow hall), or during a perceived display of dominance by the owner (such as petting, grooming, scolding, or leading). Dogs may act more aggressively toward family members than strangers, and treat the family members in a dominant way, such as walking stiffly, staring, standing over them, and ignoring commands. Punishment usually only elicits further aggression.

Dominance aggression is more common in males than females, and occasionally (but not always) castration can help. Your veterinarian

can give your intact (un-neutered) male dog a drug that will temporarily cause his hormonal state to be that of a neutered dog as a test to see if castration might help. Spaying a female will not help (and may even hinder) curing dominance aggression.

Owners of such dogs inevitably feel guilty, and wonder "Where did I go wrong?" The fault is not entirely theirs. Although some actions of the owner may have helped create the problem, these same actions would not have produced dominance aggression in dogs that were not already predisposed to the problem. In predisposed dogs, owners who act in ways to foster the dog's opinion of himself as king can lead to problems. What would convince a dog that he ranked over a person? Actions such as:

*Most Jack Russells are sweet—if mischievous—companions.*

✔ petting the dog on demand
✔ feeding the dog before eating your own meal
✔ allowing the dog to go first through doorways
✔ allowing the dog to win at games
✔ allowing the dog to have his way when he acts aggressively
✔ fearing the dog
✔ not punishing the dog for initial instances of aggression.

Treatment consists of putting the dog in his place, without direct confrontations. A popular training method from several years ago was the "alpha roll," in which you roll the dominant dog over on his back into a submissive position. However, this is a good way to get bitten and most canine behaviorists now think it is a bad idea.

It's best to avoid situations that might lead to a showdown. If, however, your dog only growls, and *never* bites, you may be able to nip the behavior in the bud before you get nipped yourself by scolding or physically correcting the dog. If your dog is likely to bite, but you still want to try, talk to your veterinarian about temporary drug therapy to calm him sufficiently during initial training, and consider having your dog wear a muzzle.

With a dominant-aggressive dog, you must cease and desist any of your behaviors that tell the dog he is the boss. As much pleasure as you may get from petting your dog absent-mindedly as you watch TV, you can't. There will be no more free lunches, and no more free pets, for your dog. From now on, your dog must work for his petting, his praise, and even his food. The work will be simple—just obeying simple commands from you. He must sit when you tell him to sit and wait until you have gone through doorways first. When he thrusts his head into your lap to be petted, you must ignore him. When you want to pet him, you must first have him obey some simple commands, and then pet him sparingly as a reward. Yes, it's tough love—but it may be your misguided tyrant's only chance.

## Housesoiling

There are many reasons why an adult dog might soil the house:

✔ Commonly, the dog was never completely housebroken to start with, and you must begin housebreaking all over again.

*Extreme submissive pose.*

✔ Sometimes a housebroken dog will be forced to soil the house because of a bout of diarrhea, and afterwards will continue to soil in the same area. If this happens, restrict that area from the dog, and revert to basic housebreaking lessons once again. Remember to thoroughly clean the areas with a deodorizer (available at pet stores) to eliminate the odor.

✔ Submissive dogs may urinate upon greeting you; punishment only makes this "submissive urination" worse. For these dogs, keep greetings calm, don't bend over or otherwise dominate the dog, and usually this can be outgrown.

✔ Some dogs defecate or urinate due to the stress of separation anxiety; you must treat the anxiety to cure the symptom.

✔ Older dogs may simply not have the bladder control that they had as youngsters; paper training or a doggy door is the best solution for them.

✔ Older spayed females may "dribble"; ask your veterinarian about estrogen supplementation that may help.

✔ Dogs may have lost control due to a bladder infection; several small urine spots (especially if bloody or dark) are a sign that a trip to the veterinarian is needed.

✔ Male dogs may "lift their leg" inside the house as a means of marking it as theirs. Castration will usually solve this problem; otherwise, diligent deodorizing and the use of some dog-deterring odorants (available at pet stores) may help.

## A Dog's-eye View

How can you train a dog if you can't communicate with him? And how do you communicate with a member of another species when you live in two very different sensory worlds? In order to see eye-to-eye with your JRT, you need to understand the world he lives in and the way he talks.

Like their wolf ancestors, Jack Russells depend upon facial expressions and body language in social interactions:

✔ A yawn is often a sign of nervousness.

✔ Drooling and panting can indicate extreme nervousness (or carsickness).

✔ The combination of a wagging tail, lowered head, and exposed teeth upon greeting is a sign of submission.

✔ The combination of a lowered body, wagging tucked tail, urination, and perhaps even rolling over is a sign of extreme submission.

✔ The combination of exposed teeth, a high, rigidly held tail, raised hackles, very upright posture, stiff-legged gait, direct stare, forward raised ears, and perhaps leg lifting to urinate indicates very dominant, possibly threatening behavior.

✔ The combination of a wagging tail, front legs and elbows on the ground, and rear in the air, with or without vocalizations is the classic "play-bow" position, and is an invitation for a game.

*The classic "play-bow" position.*

Your JRT not only speaks a different language than you do, but he lives in a different sensory world.

✔ **Olfaction:** The dog's scenting ability is so vastly superior to ours that it is as though we were blind in comparison. The dog can seek out hidden objects and animals, follow a trail for miles, and distinguish between individuals by scent. The JRT is a particularly adept scenter, and you would do well to trust his nose.

✔ **Taste:** Dogs also have a well-developed sense of taste, and have most of the same taste receptors that we do. Research has shown that they prefer meat (not exactly earthshaking news!), and while there are many individual differences, the average dog prefers beef, pork, lamb, chicken, and horsemeat, in that order. Of course, JRTs sometimes seem to prefer anything in reach!

Dogs have sugar receptors similar to ours, which explains why many have a sweet tooth. But their perception of artificial sweeteners is not like ours, and they seem to taste bitter to them.

✔ **Vision:** No dogs see the world with as much detail or color as do humans. The dog's sense of color is similar to that of what is commonly called a "color-blind" person, which is not really blind to color at all. That is, they confuse similar shades of yellow-green, yellow, orange, and red, but can readily see and discriminate blue, indigo, and violet from all other colors and each other.

The dog's eye is superior when it comes to seeing in very dim light. The eyeshine you may see from your dog's eyes at night is from a reflective structure (the tapetum lucidum) that serves to increase its ability to see in very dim light, and the dog has a greater proportion of the type of retinal cells (rods) that are highly sensitive to dim light than humans have. Your JRT is very much at home in the near dark.

✔ **Hearing:** Dogs can hear much higher tones than can humans and can be irritated by high hums from your TV or from those ultrasonic flea collars. The high-pitched "dog whistles," so popular years ago, emit a tone higher than humans can hear, but well within the dog's range. Dogs need to be trained to respond to these whistles just as they would any other command or signal. A problem is that owners can't tell when the whistle malfunctions.

Ultrasonic training devices now available emit a high-frequency sound inaudible to us, but irritating and distracting to dogs. They can be a useful training aid for disrupting unwanted behavior, but only if accompanied by rewarding the dog for correct behavior.

✔ **Pain:** Many people erroneously believe that animals cannot feel pain, but common sense

*The Jack Russell makes use of all its senses when exploring the wilds.*

and scientific research indicate that dogs and other animals have a well-developed sense of pain. Many dogs are amazingly stoic, however, and their ability to deal with pain is not totally understood at present. Because a dog may not be able to express that he is in pain, you must be alert to changes in your dog's demeanor. A stiff gait, low head carriage, reluctance to get up, irritability, dilated pupils, whining, or limping are all indications that your dog is in pain.

## Hit the Road

A car trip with your JRT can be a rewarding experience, as the two of you join together for an adventurous odyssey. A dog gives you a good excuse to stop and enjoy the scenery up close, and maybe even get some exercise along the way.

A trip with your JRT can also be a nightmare, as you are turned away from motels, parks, attractions, and beaches. The moral? Make plans. Several books are available listing establishments that accept pets. (Look in your library

or book store.) Call ahead to attractions to see if they have arrangements for pets.

The number of establishments that accept pets decreases yearly. You can thank dog owners who seem to think their little "Rascal" is above the law, owners who let Rascal defecate on sidewalks, beaches, and playgrounds, bark himself hoarse in the motel room, and leave behind wet spots on the carpet and chew marks on the chairs.

Luckily some places still remain where pets are welcome. Schedule several stops in places your Jack Russell can enjoy. If you are driving, bring a long retractable lead so your dog can stretch his legs safely every few hours along the way. Keep an eye out for little nature excursions, which are wonderful for refreshing both dog and owner. But always do so with a cautious eye; never risk your own or your dog's safety by stopping in totally desolate locales, no matter how breathtaking the view.

## The Doggy Seat Belt

Ideally your JRT should always ride with the equivalent of a doggy seat belt: the cage. Not only can a cage help to prevent accidents by keeping your dog from using your lap as a trampoline, but, if an accident does happen, a cage can save your dog's life. A cage with a padlocked door can also be useful when you need to leave the dog in the car with the windows partly down.

## Airplane Trips

Although car trips are the most common mode of travel for dogs, sometimes an airplane trip is required (note that dogs are not allowed on trains). Small dogs are often able to ride in the passenger cabin of an airplane, if their cage can fit under the seat. Always opt for this choice if available. When making reservations ask what type of cage you must have.

If you must ship a dog by himself, it is better to ship "counter to counter" than as regular air cargo, and note the following:

✔ Make sure the cage is secure, and for good measure put an elastic "bungee" band around the cage door.

✔ Don't feed your dog before traveling. The cage should have a small dish that can be attached to the door. The night before the trip fill it with water and freeze it; as it melts during the flight, the dog will have water that otherwise would have spilled out during the loading process.

✔ Include a large chewbone to occupy your jet-setter.

*A traveling cage keeps your JRT safe and secure when away from home.*

✔ Be sure to line the cage with soft, absorbent material, preferably something that can be thrown away if soiled.

✔ Although air compartments are heated, they are not air-conditioned, and in hot weather dogs have been known to overheat while the plane was still on the runway. Never ship in the heat of day.

## The Perfect Guest

Whether you will be spending your nights at a motel, campground, or even a friend's home, always have your dog on his very best behavior. Ask beforehand if it will be OK for you to bring your Jack Russell. Have your dog clean and parasite free. Do not allow your dog to run helter-skelter through the homes of friends. Bring your dog's own clean blanket or bed, or better yet, his cage. Your JRT will appreciate the familiar place to sleep, and your friends and motel owners will breathe sighs of relief. Even though your dog may be accustomed to sleeping on furniture at home, a proper canine guest stays on the floor when visiting. Walk and walk your dog (and clean up after him ) to make sure no accidents occur inside. If they do, clean them immediately. Don't leave any surprises for your hosts! Changes in water or food, or simply stress can often result in diarrhea, so be particularly attentive to taking your dog out often. *Never, never* leave your dog unattended in a strange place. The dog's perception is that you have left and forgotten him; he either barks or tries to dig his way out through the doors and windows in an effort to find you, or becomes upset and relieves himself on the carpet. Always remember that anyone who allows your dog to spend the night is doing so with a certain amount of trepidation; make sure your JRT is so well behaved that you are both invited back.

## The JRT's Travel Case

Your JRT should have his own travel case that should include:

✔ first aid kit

✔ heartworm preventative and any other medications, especially antidiarrhea medication

✔ food and water bowls

✔ some dog biscuits and chewies

✔ flea spray

✔ flea comb and brush

✔ bedding

✔ short and long leashes

✔ sweater for cold weather

✔ flashlight for night walks

✔ plastic baggies or other poop disposal means

✔ moist towelettes, paper towels, and self-rinse shampoo

✔ food (the type the dog is used to eating, to avoid stomach upsets)

✔ dog tags, including license tags and a tag indicating where you could be reached while on your trip, or including the address of someone you know will be at home

✔ recent color photo in case your JRT somehow gets lost

✔ health and rabies certificates

✔ bottled water or water from home (many dogs are very sensitive to changes in water and can develop diarrhea).

With a little foresight you may find your Jack Russell to be the most entertaining and enjoyable travel companion you could invite along. And don't be surprised if you find your dog nestled in your suitcase among your packed clothes!

Even if the only trip you take with your JRT is around the block, please, for the sake of dog ownership in the future, maintain the same high standards that you would if traveling:

✔ Always clean up after your dog. Carry a little plastic bag for disposal later.

✔ Don't let your dog run loose where he could bother picnickers, bicyclists, joggers, or children.

✔ Never let your dog bark unchecked.

✔ Never let your dog jump up on people.

✔ Never take a chance of your dog biting anybody.

✔ Don't allow your JRT to lunge at other dogs.

## Home Away from Home

Sometimes you must leave your dog behind when you travel. Ask friends or your veterinarian for boarding kennel recommendations.

### Kennels

The ideal kennel will be approved by the American Boarding Kennel Association, have climate-controlled accommodations, and keep your JRT either indoors or in a combination indoor/outdoor run. Make an unannounced visit to the kennel and ask to see the facilities. While you can't expect spotlessness and a perfumy atmosphere, most runs should be clean and the odor should not be overpowering. All dogs should have clean water and at least some bedding. Good kennels will require proof of immunizations and an incoming check for fleas. They will allow you to bring toys and bedding, and will administer prescribed medication. Strange dogs should not be allowed to mingle, and the entire kennel area should be fenced.

### Pet-sitters

Your dog may be more comfortable if an experienced pet-sitter or responsible friend comes to your home and feeds and exercises your dog regularly. This works best if you have a doggy door. The kid next door is seldom a good choice for this important responsibility. It is too easy for the dog to slip out the door, or for signs of illness to go unnoticed, unless the sitter is an experienced dog person.

Whatever means you choose, always leave emergency numbers and your veterinarian's name. Make arrangements with your veterinarian to treat your dog for any problems that may arise. This means leaving a written agreement stating that you give permission for treatment and accept responsibility for charges.

## Little Dog Lost

Never leave your dog in a place where he would be vulnerable to a Jack Russell hijack, and never be complacent about your dog's absence. If your JRT escapes or gets lost, you must act quickly in order to ensure his safe return.

✔ Start your search at the very worst place you could imagine him going, usually the nearest highway. Don't drive recklessly and endanger your own dog's life should he run across the road.

✔ If you still can't find your pet, get pictures of your dog and go door to door; ask any workers or delivery persons in the area.

✔ Search for any burrows that your JRT may be exploring. Some dogs have been lost for days only to be found underground with a cornered animal.

✔ Call the local animal control, police department, and veterinarians.

✔ If your dog is tattooed, contact the tattoo registry.

✔ Make up *large* posters with a picture of a JRT.

✔ Take out an ad in the local paper. Mention a reward, but do not specify an amount.

*Ever ready for a journey, no matter how large or small . . .*

Never give anyone reward money before seeing your dog. There are a number of scams involving answering lost dog ads, many asking for money for shipping the dog back to you from a distance or for paying vet bills, when very often these people have not really found your dog. If your dog is tattooed, you can have the person read the number to you in order to positively identify him.

## Identification

Even license tags cannot always ensure your dog's return, because they must be on the dog to be effective. Tattooing your social security number or your dog's registration number on the inside of his thigh provides a permanent means of identification; these numbers can be registered with one of the several lost pet recovery agencies. Microchips are now available that are placed under the dog's skin with a simple

injection. They contain information about the dog and cannot be removed, but require a special scanner (owned by most animal shelters) to be read (see Information, page 111). You may wish to discuss this option with your veterinarian or local breeders.

## The Friend of a Lifetime

You have a lifetime of experiences to share with your new Jack Russell Terrier. The remainder of your dog's life will be spent under your care and guidance. Your life may change dramatically in the years to come: marriage, divorce, new baby, new home—for better or worse, your dog will still depend on you and still love you. Always remember the promise you made to yourself and your future puppy before you made the commitment to share your life: to keep your interest in your dog and care for him every day of his life with as much love and enthusiasm as you did the first day he arrived home.

# MIND GAMES

Part of the current appeal of the JRT has arisen from its frequent television appearances, leading to the perception that JRTs are easy to train. Not necessarily! Some of the most talented JRT stars were actually intolerable as pets and were initially obedience school dropouts! In the hands of professional dog trainers, such canine delinquents, always in motion and perpetually inquisitive, make the best show biz candidates. This is because it is easier to train a dog *when* to do something than it is to train one *how* to do something.

Dog training methods have changed little through the years—but they should have. Traditional dog training methods based on force are the least successful and most widespread. The problem with training by force is that it relies upon punishment as a means of telling the dog what *not* to do, but it is seldom successful in telling the dog what he *should* do.

In some ways, dogs learn like people do, meaning they learn best when training is combined with other interests. What are a Jack Russell's interests? For most of them, it's food, hunting, and games. Hunting may be a bit difficult to integrate into everyday training, but food and games are not.

## Food for Thought

Many years ago the idea was perpetuated that dogs should never be trained with food.

*Jack Russells are natural show-offs.*

Yet professional animal trainers and animal learning scientists all knew that food training produced excellent results because food tells the animal what behaviors are correct. Only recently has food-motivated training become accepted in training the family dog, and owners are finding that dogs learn faster, mind more reliably, work more eagerly, and have a more trusting dog-owner relationship.

JRTs often have a "What's in it for me?" attitude, and food provides them with a satisfactory answer. At first food is used to guide the dog by the nose until he is in the desired position, before rewarding him. After the dog knows what is expected, the food is held out of sight and only given to the dog when he has performed correctly. Ultimately, the dog is weaned from getting a food reward each time, but still gets one every once in a while. Such a random payoff schedule has been shown to be very effective in both animals and humans (as in slot machine payoffs!).

The idea of bribing our dogs with food runs counter to the idealized picture of Lassie obeying out of pure goodness and love. But the real Lassie, of course, was performing for food rewards. Dog owners have been told for years that the dog should work for praise alone, but praise alone is not really a terribly strong motivator for most dogs, and even worse for most JRTs. Praise can become a stronger motivator by always praising immediately before the food reward is given. In this way it becomes a secondary reinforcer, much as a gold star on a child's schoolwork gains reinforcing value because it has been paired with other positive reinforcement. Eventually, the dog can be weaned from the food and will come to work in large part for praise, but food should still be given as a reward intermittently.

## All in the Timing

The first ingredient in any command is your dog's name. You probably spend a good deal of your day talking, with very few words intended as commands for your dog. So warn your terrier that this talk is directed toward him.

Many trainers make the mistake of saying the command word *at the same time* that they are placing the dog into position. *This is incorrect.* The command comes immediately *before* the desired action or position. The crux of training is anticipation. The dog comes to anticipate that, after hearing a command, he will be induced to perform some action, and he will eventually perform this action without further assistance from you. On the other hand, when the command and action come at the same time, not only does the dog tend to pay more attention to your action of placing him in position, and less attention to the command word, but the command word loses

its predictive value for the dog. Remember: Name, command, action, reward!

**Clicker Training:** Professional dog trainers go one step further. They use a signal (such as a click sound) to instantly tell the dog when he has performed correctly. The signal is then followed by a food reward. A clicker signal is used because it is fast, noticeable, and something the dog otherwise does not encounter in everyday life. In order to apply this technique to the following instructions, whenever giving a reward is mentioned, you should precede it with a clicker signal. Even if you don't use a clicker, always precede any tangible reward with "*Good!*" and praise.

## Terrier Training Tips

JRTs are highly intelligent but can be a handful unless trained properly. To live in peace with your JRT use the same training techniques that the professionals use. Remember the following rules of terrier training:

✔ **Guide, don't force:** JRTs want to please you but they also want to please themselves. They are especially poor candidates for force training, and don't take well to being bullied into submission. Tough, domineering training techniques are more likely to bring out the stubborn streak in a JRT. In a battle of wills, the JRT will usually win.

✔ **Correct, don't punish:** Such methods as striking, shaking, choking, and even hanging have been touted by some (stupid) trainers. Do not try them! They are

*Toys can be an excellent reward for young JRTs.*

*Teach stationary exercises on a raised surface for added control.*

extremely dangerous, counterproductive, and cruel. They have no place in the training of a beloved family member—plus, they don't work. Remember, JRTs are bred to continue on in the face of adversity.

✔ **Correct and be done with it:** Owners sometimes try to make this "a correction the dog will remember" by ignoring the dog for the rest of the day. The dog may indeed remember that his owner ignored him, but he will not remember why. The dog can only relate its present behavior to your actions.

✔ **You get what you ask for:** Dogs repeat actions that bring them rewards, whether you intend for them to or not. Feeding your JRT to make him be quiet might work momentarily, but in the long run you will end up with a noisier dog, because your JRT learns that barking brings food. Make sure you reward only those behaviors you want to see more often.

✔ **Mean what you say:** Sometimes a Jack Russell can be awfully cute when he misbehaves, or sometimes your hands are full, and sometimes you just aren't sure what you want from your dog. But lapses in consistency are ultimately unfair to the dog. If you feed your JRT from the table because he begs "just this one time," you have taught him that while begging may not always result in a handout, you never know, it just might pay off tonight. In other words, you have taught your dog to beg.

✔ **Say what you mean:** Your JRT takes his commands literally. If you have taught that *down* means to lie down, then what must the dog think when you yell *"Down"* to tell him to get off the sofa where he was already lying

down? Or *"Sit down"* when you mean *"Sit?"* If *stay* means not to move until given a release word, and you say *"Stay here"* as you leave the house for work, do you really want your dog to sit by the door all day until you get home?

✔ **Train before meals:** Your JRT will work better if his stomach is not full, and will be more responsive to food rewards. Never try to train a sleepy, tired, or hot JRT.

✔ **Happy endings:** Begin and end each training session with something the dog can do well. And keep sessions short and fun—no longer than 10 to 15 minutes. Dogs have short attention spans and you will notice that after about 15 minutes their performance will begin to suffer unless a lot of play is involved. To continue to train a tired or bored dog will result in the training of bad habits, resentment in the dog, and frustration for the trainer.

Especially when training a young puppy, or when you only have one or two different exercises to practice, quit while you are ahead! Keep your JRT wanting more, and you will have a happy, willing, obedience partner.

✔ **Once is enough:** Repeating a command over and over, or shouting it louder and louder, never helped anyone, dog or human, understand what is expected of them. Your JRT is not hard of hearing.

✔ **Think like a dog:** Dogs live in the present; if you punish them they can only assume it is for their behavior at the time of punishment. So if you discover a mess, and drag your dog to it from his nap in the other room, and scold, the impression to the dog will be that either he is being scolded for napping, or that his owner is mentally unstable. In many ways dogs are like young children; they act to gratify themselves,

*It's easier to teach a dog to lie down if you do so on a blanket at first.*

and they often do so without thinking ahead to consequences. But, unlike young children, dogs cannot understand human language (except for those words you teach them), so you cannot explain to them that their actions of five minutes earlier were bad. Remember, timing is everything in a correction. If you discover your dog in the process of having an "accident," and snatch the dog up and deposit him outside, and then yell *"No,"* your dog can only conclude that you have yelled *"No"* to him for eliminating outside. Correct timing would be *"No,"* quickly take the dog outside, and then reward him once he eliminates outside. In this way you have corrected the dog's undesired behavior and helped the dog understand desired behavior.

✔ **The best laid plans:** Finally, nothing will ever go just as perfectly as it seems to in all of the training instructions but, although there may be setbacks, you can train your dog, as long as you remember to be consistent, firm, gentle, realistic, and most of all, patient.

# Training Equipment

Equipment for training should include a 6-foot (1.8-m) and a 20-foot (6-m) lightweight lead. For puppies it is convenient to use one of the lightweight adjustable-size show leads. Some JRTs can be trained with a buckle collar, but a choke collar is also an acceptable choice as long as you know how to use it correctly.

*A choke collar is not for choking!* The proper way to administer a correction with a choke collar is with a gentle snap, then immediate release. If you think the point of the correction is to startle the dog by the sound of the chain links moving, rather than to choke or in any way hurt your dog, you will be correcting with the right level of force. The choke collar is placed on the dog so that the ring with the lead attached comes up around the left side of the dog's neck, and through the other ring. If put on backwards, it will not release itself after being tightened (since you will be on the right side of your dog for most training). The choke collar should *never* be left on your Jack Russell after a training session; there are too many tragic cases where a choke collar really did earn its name after being snagged on a fence, bush, or even a playmate's

*The correct placement of the choke collar is with the long end (to which the lead is attached) coming over the top of the dog's head from the dog's left to right side.*

tooth. Allowing a dog to run around wearing a choke collar is like allowing a child to run around wearing a hangman's noose.

# Teaching Your JRT to Heel

Introduce your pup to wearing a lightweight leash with lots of patience and praise. Walking alongside of you on lead is a new experience for a youngster, and many will freeze in their tracks once they discover their freedom is being violated. In this case, don't simply drag him, but instead coax him with food. When he follows you, praise and reward him. He thus comes to realize that following you while walking on lead pays off.

Most JRTs have a tendency to forge ahead, pulling their hapless owners behind them, zigzagging from bush to fencepost. Although at times this may be acceptable to you, at other times it will be annoying and perhaps even dangerous. Even if you have no intention of teaching a perfect competition *heel,* you

need to teach it as a way of letting your JRT know it's your turn to be the leader.

**Tip:** A leash that comes from several feet overhead has virtually no guiding ability whatsoever. You need a lower pivot point for the leash in relation to the dog, and you can achieve this by what is called a "solid leash." This is simply a hollow, light tube, such as PVC pipe, about 3 feet (91 cm) long, through which you string your leash. Also, to prevent your dog from sitting or lying down, loop part of your regular leash around his belly and hold onto that part, so you have a convenient "handle."

## The Heel Position

Using the solid leash, have your JRT sit in the *heel* position; that is, on your left side with his neck next to and parallel with your leg. Say "*Wolfman, heel*" and step off with your left foot first. (In contrast, step off on your right foot when you leave your dog on a *stay*. If you are consistent, the foot that moves first will provide an eye-level cue for your little dog.)

During your first few practice sessions you will keep your dog on a short lead, holding him in *heel* position, and of course praising him. The traditional method of letting the dog lunge to the end of the lead and then snapping him back is unfair if you haven't first shown the dog what is expected of him. Instead, after a few sessions of showing the dog the *heel* position, give him a little more loose lead and use a tidbit to guide him into correct position. If your JRT still forges ahead after you have shown him what is expected, pull him back to position with a quick, gentle tug of the lead, then release.

If, after a few days' practice, your dog still seems oblivious to your efforts, then turn unexpectedly several times. This will result in a jerk to your dog, but don't feel too guilty—you tried to show him the right path. Give your dog a chance to *heel* in position before resort-

*Nobody said the sit-stay was a Jack Russell's favorite exercise!*

*Any naturally occurring behavior can be turned into a trick by carefully timed rewards.*

ing to another unexpected turn. Your dog will learn that you can be unpredictable, and if he wants to avoid the jerk, he had better keep an eye on you and remain by your side. Be fore-warned that if you use this correction too often, you will create an unhappy heeler that continually lags behind you in order to keep you in his line of sight.

**Tip:** Keep up a pace that requires your JRT to walk fairly briskly; too slow a pace gives dogs time to sniff, look all around, and in general become distracted; a brisk pace will focus the dog's attention upon you and generally aid training.

### Variations

As you progress you will want to add some right, left, and about-faces, and walk at all different speeds. Then practice in different areas (still always on-lead) and around different distractions. You can teach your JRT to sit every time you stop. Vary your routine to combat boredom, and keep training sessions short. Be sure to give the *OK* command before allowing your dog to sniff, forge, and meander on lead.

## Tricks and Treats

The only problem with basic obedience skills is that they don't exactly astound your friends. For that you need something flashy, some incredible feat of intelligence and dexterity: a dog trick. Try the standards: *roll over, play dead,*

*catch, sit up, speak.* All are easy to teach with the help of the same obedience concepts outlined in the training section. Teach *roll over* by giving the command when the dog is already on his back, then guide him the rest of the way over with a treat. Teach speak by saying *"Speak"* when it appears your JRT is about to bark. Teach *catch* by throwing a tidbit or other item your dog wants; when it lands on the ground, snatch it up before your dog can. Your dog will quickly figure out the only way to get it is to grab it in midair! If your dog can physically do it, you can teach him when to do it. The success of JRTs as animal actors shows how adept they are at learning tricks of all sorts.

It's never too early or too late to start the education of your Jack Russell Terrier. With a very young JRT, train for short time periods. By the time your JRT pup (here named "Wolfman") reaches six months of age, he should be familiar with several necessary commands.

Following are the most important commands your JRT should know:

## Watch Me

A common problem when training any dog is that the dog's attention is elsewhere. You can teach your dog to pay attention to you by teaching him the *watch me* command. Say "*Wolfman, watch me,*" and when he looks in your direction, give him a treat or other reward.

Gradually require him to look at you for longer and longer periods before rewarding him. Teach *watch me* before going on to the other commands.

**Tip:** Teach stationary exercises on a tabletop or other raised surface. This allows you to have eye contact with your dog and gives you a better vantage from which to help your dog learn.

## Sit

Because JRTs are already close to the ground, many of them virtually teach themselves to sit as a means of being more comfortable while looking up at you. But you can hasten the process by holding a tidbit above your puppy's eye level, saying "*Wolfman, sit,*" and then moving the tidbit toward him

until it's slightly behind and above his eyes. You may have to keep a hand on his rump to prevent him from jumping up. When he begins to look up and bend his hind legs, praise, then offer the tidbit. Repeat this, requiring him to bend his legs more and more until he must be sitting before receiving praise.

**Tip:** To train your dog at your feet, extend your arm length with a back scratcher with which to guide and even pet your dog without having to bend over.

## Stay

A dangerous habit of many dogs is to bolt through open doors, whether they are in the house or car. Teach your dog to sit and stay until given the release signal before walking through the front door or exiting your car.

Have your dog sit, then say "*Stay*" in a soothing voice. (For commands in which the dog is not supposed to move, don't precede the command with the dog's name, because the dog tends to jump up in anticipation of doing something.) If your JRT attempts to get up or lie down, gently but instantly place him back into position. After the first few tries you'll quickly understand how a Jack-in-the-Box got its

*Use food to guide your dog's head backwards and slightly up. If you position his rear end next to a wall, he will have to sit in order to reach the treat.*

name, but eventually your Jack Russell will forget and leave his rear on the ground for a few seconds. Reward! Then work up to a few seconds, give a release word (*"OK!"*), praise, and give a tidbit. Next, step out (starting with your right foot) and turn to stand directly in front of your dog while he stays. Work up to longer times, but don't ask a young puppy to stay longer than 30 seconds. The object is not to push your dog to the limit, but to let him succeed. To do this you must be very patient, and you must increase your times and distances in very small increments. Finally, practice with the dog on lead by the front door or in the car. For a reward, take him for a walk!

**Tip:** Don't stare at your dog during the *stay*, as this is perceived by the dog as a threat. Staring can cause a dog to squirm out of position or creep to you submissively.

## Come

Coming on command is more than a cute trick—it could save your dog's life. Your puppy probably already knows how to come; after all, he comes when he sees you with the food bowl, or perhaps with the leash or a favorite toy. You may have even used the word *"Come"* to get his attention then. If so, you have a head start. You want your puppy to respond to *"Wolfman, come"* with the same enthusiasm as though you were setting down his supper; in other words, *"Come"* should always be associated with good things.

**Tip:** Never have your dog come to you and then scold him for something. In the dog's mind, he is being scolded for coming, not for any earlier misdeed.

The best time to start is when your JRT is a young puppy, but it's never too late. You will need a helper and an enclosed area, such as a

*Getting down to dog level can encourage a reluctant dog to come.*

hallway. Entice the pup while your helper holds him. When the pup is struggling to get to you, call *"Wolfman, come!"* with great enthusiasm, at the same time turning around and running away. Your helper should then release the pup so he chases after you. When he catches you, reward him with play and a treat. Next move your training outdoors with a long line. If he ignores you for more than a second, tug on the lead to get his attention, but don't drag him. Response to the *come* command is not one that can be put off until your dog feels like coming. In addition, the longer you separate the tug from the command, the harder it will be for your pup to relate the two, and in the long run, the harder the training will be on the youngster. After the tug, be sure to run backwards and make the pup think that it was all part of the grand game. You should ultimately practice (on lead) in the presence of distractions, such as other leashed dogs, unfamiliar people, cats, and cars.

**Tip:** Have your JRT sit in front of you before getting the tidbit in order to prevent the annoying habit some dogs have of dancing around just beyond your reach.

# HEALTH FOOD

"You are what you eat" is just as true for dogs as it is for people. Because your JRT can't go shopping for her dinner, she "will be what you feed her," so you have total responsibility for feeding your dog a high-quality balanced diet that will enable her to live a long and active life. Dog food claims can be conflicting and confusing, but there are some guidelines that you can use when selecting a proper diet for your Jack Russell Terrier.

## Meat and Potatoes

Although dogs are members of the order Carnivora ("meateaters"), they are actually omnivorous, meaning their nutritional needs can be met by a diet derived from both animals and plants. Most dogs do have a decided preference for meat over non-meat foods, but a balanced meal will combine both meat and plant-based nutrients:

✔ **Dry food** (containing about 10 percent moisture) is the most popular, economical, and healthy, but least palatable form of dog food.

✔ **Semimoist foods** (with about 30 percent moisture) contain high levels of sugar used as preservatives. They are palatable and convenient, and very handy for traveling. Semimoist foods are not a very good nutritional choice, and can result in excessive water consumption,

*Good food will help your JRT reach great heights.*

leading to excessive urination. Pay no attention to their meat-like shapes; they all start out as a powder and are formed to look like meat chunks or ground beef.

✔ **Canned food** has a high moisture content (about 75 percent), which helps to make them tasty, but it also makes them comparatively expensive, since you are in essence buying water. A steady diet of canned food would not provide the chewing necessary to maintain dental health, although supplementation with chew sticks, nylon bones, and dog biscuits can provide the necessary chewing action. Most people mix canned and dry food for the best of both worlds.

✔ **Dog biscuits** provide excellent chewing action, and some of the better varieties provide complete nutrition. They are convenient for snacks and travel.

✔ **Homemade diets** are available that combine fresh ingredients at proper levels. Feeding a dog a homemade or fresh diet entails more than concocting your own recipes. Find a reputable source of recipes designed by a canine nutritionist if you elect to make your own dog food.

✔ **Raw diets** are currently popular with many people who feel it is a more natural and healthful way to feed. Note, however, that the domestic dog has not been a wild canid for many generations, and that they may have lost some of the mechanisms that protected them from foodborne disease. In addition, wild canids caught and ate their own food, whereas much of the raw food available in this country comes from meat processing plants in which diseases such as salmonella are rampant. Dogs are not as susceptible to salmonella or *E. coli* as people are, but they can still get sick from them on occasion. If you elect to feed raw foods, know your source!

## Nutrient Levels

The Association of American Feed Control Officials (AAFCO) has recommended minimal nutrient levels for dogs based upon controlled feeding studies.

Feed a high-quality food from a name-brand company. Dog owners tend to be one of three types when it comes to feeding their dogs: the first tries to save money by feeding dog food made from sawdust and corncobs, and then wonders why the dog has to eat so much of it; the other extreme chooses a food because it costs the most and is made from bee pollen, llama milk, and caviar yolk (and of course, no preservatives) and then wonders why the food is rancid half the time and their dog is a blimp; and the third type buys a high-quality food from a recognized source that has proven their food through actual

feeding trials. Avoid food that has been sitting on the shelf for long periods, or that has holes in the bag or grease that has seeped through the bag.

Finally, find a food that your terrier enjoys. Mealtime is a highlight of a dog's day. Although a dog will eventually eat even the most unsavory of dog food if given no choice, it hardly seems fair to deprive your family member of one of life's simple and, for a dog, most important, pleasures.

**A word of caution:** Dogs will often seem to prefer a new food when it is first offered, but this may simply be due to its novelty. Only after you buy a six-month supply of this alleged canine ambrosia will you discover it was just a passing fancy—one more reason you should never buy a lot of dog food at once.

# Read the Label!

When comparing food labels, keep in mind that differences in moisture content make it difficult to make direct comparisons between the guaranteed analyses in various forms of food. The components that vary most from one brand of food to another are protein and fat percentages.

**Protein:** Many high-quality foods boast of being high in protein, and with good reason. Protein provides the necessary building blocks for growth and maintenance of bones, muscle, and coat, and in the production of infection fighting antibodies. Meat-derived protein is more highly digestible than plant-derived protein, and is of higher quality. The quality of protein is as important as the quantity of protein.

*Meals should be healthy and tasty.*

*A JRT pup will need a diet high in protein.*

Puppies and adolescents need particularly high protein levels in their diets, which is one reason they should be fed a food formulated for their life stage. Older dogs, especially those with kidney problems, should be fed lower levels of very high-quality protein. Recent studies have also shown that higher levels of protein (about 24 percent dry matter) are essential in maintaining lean body mass when on a weight-loss diet. If your JRT is active throughout the day, or is underweight, you may want to feed her a high-quality protein food. Most JRT housedogs will do fine on regular adult foods having protein levels of about 20 percent (dry food percentage).

**Fat:** Fat is the calorie-rich component of foods, and most dogs prefer the taste of foods with higher fat content. Fat is necessary to good health, aiding in the transport of important vitamins and providing energy. Dogs deficient in fat often have sparse, dry coats. A higher fat content is usually found in puppy foods, while obese dogs or dogs with heart problems should be fed a lower fat food. Many high-protein foods also have a high fat content.

Choose a food that has a protein and fat content best suited for your dog's life stage, adjusting for any weight or health problems (prescription diets formulated for specific health problems are available). Also examine the list of ingredients: A good rule of thumb is that three or four of the first six ingredients should be animal derived. These tend to be more palatable and more highly digestible than plant-based ingredients; more highly digestible foods mean less stool volume and fewer gas problems.

You may have to do a little experimenting to find just the right food, but a word of warning: One of the great mysteries of life is why a species, such as the dog, that is known for its lead stomach and preference to eat out of garbage cans, can at the same time develop violently upset stomachs simply from changing from one high-quality dog food to another. But it happens. So when changing foods you should do so gradually, mixing in progressively more and more of the new food each day for several days.

## Fill'er Up?

The dog's wild ancestor, the wolf, evolved to survive feast and famine, gorging following a kill but then perhaps waiting several days before another feast. In today's world, dogs can feast daily and without the period of famine can easily become obese.

Very young puppies should be fed three or four times a day, on a regular schedule. Feed them as much as they want to eat in about 15 minutes. From the age of three to six months, pups should be fed three times daily; after that, twice daily. Adult dogs can be fed once a day, but it is actually preferable to feed smaller meals twice a day.

*It's so hard to say "no more" to hungry eyes, so try some low-calorie treats.*

Some people let the dog decide when to eat by leaving food available at all times. This is usually not a good idea, as many dogs overindulge or become possessive, and anything but dry food will spoil.

## Fat Jacks

A JRT in proper weight should have ribs that can just be felt when you run your hands along the rib cage. Viewed from above, she should have an hourglass figure. There should be no roll of fat over the withers or rump.

If your JRT is overweight, switch to one of the commercially available high-fiber and low-fat, diet dog foods that supply about 15 percent fewer calories per pound. It is preferable to feed one of these foods rather than simply feeding less of a high-calorie food. Make sure family members aren't sneaking the dog forbidden tidbits.

Many people find that one of the many pleasures of dog ownership is sharing a special treat with their pet. Rather than giving up this bonding activity, substitute a low-calorie alternative such as rice cakes or carrots, or even a small cube of cooked chicken breast. Keep the dog out of the kitchen or dining area at food preparation or mealtimes. Schedule a walk immediately following your dinner to get your dog's mind off your leftovers—it will be good for both of you.

If your dog remains overweight, seek your veterinarian's opinion. Heart disease and some endocrine disorders, such as hypothyroidism or Cushing's disease, or the early stages of diabetes, can cause the appearance of obesity and should be ruled out or treated. However, most cases of obesity are simply from eating more calories than are expended. Obesity predisposes dogs to joint injuries and heart problems. The JRT is too fun loving to be burdened by a body of blubber.

## Jack Sprats

If you have an underweight dog, try feeding puppy food, adding water, milk, bouillon, or canned food, and heating the food slightly to increase aroma and palatability. Milk will cause many dogs to have diarrhea, so start with only a small amount at first. Try a couple of dog food brands, but if your JRT still won't eat, you may have to employ some tough love. Many picky eaters are created when their owners begin to spice up their food with especially tasty treats. The dog then refuses to eat unless the preferred treat is offered, and finally learns that if she refuses even that proffered treat, another even tastier enticement will be offered. Give your dog a good, tasty meal, but don't succumb to Jack Russell blackmail or you may be a slave to your dog's gastronomical whims for years to come.

Most JRTs are "easy-keepers," meaning they eat readily, are not finicky, and also seem to maintain their weight at an optimal level.

An exception is a sick dog, in which case feeding by hand is warranted. Cat food or meat baby food are both relished by dogs and may entice a dog without an appetite to eat.

*"Is that the can opener I hear?" Keep your overweight Jack away from temptation!*

# KEEPING UP APPEARANCES

Just as good maintenance makes your car look better and prolongs its running life, so does good JRT maintenance both improve the looks of your dog and, possibly, add years to his life.

## Hair of the Dog

Care of the Jack Russell jacket is simple, especially for the wash-and-wear smooth coat. Weekly brushing with a bristle brush or rubber shedding mitt, and an occasional bath will suffice for the pet. For special occasions, tidying up the few scraggly hairs under the tail, rump, abdomen, and feet is all that is required.

### Coat Care

The broken and rough coats, however, need considerably more care to retain the proper JRT appearance. If left unattended, the rough coat will grow overly long, soft, and scraggly, and the dog will lose the crisp, neat outline so typical of the JRT. This is especially true of undesirable overly long or soft coats. If the coat is clipped, it exposes the soft undercoat, resulting in a coat lacking the proper water-repelling harsh terrier texture coat. This is acceptable for most pets, but not for show dogs. In addition,

*Rub a dub dub...a miffed Jack in a tub.*

because the shafts of the dead hairs are still in place, clipping does little to make the dog ultimately more refreshed and comfortable, and you will never achieve a final neat look, because the hairs will be continually growing out and falling out.

**Plucking:** Ideally, the coat should be plucked, pulling out the longer dead hairs and allowing new harsh hair to grow back in its place. The best time to pluck, or strip, the coat is when the dog is naturally shedding, and for most pet JRTs, doing this once or (better) twice a year will suffice. Show dogs will need to be stripped more often.

A grooming table will make the process much easier, but you can also use any raised surface covered with a towel to catch the loose hair. Begin by using a slicker brush to remove any loose undercoat. Try pulling out a few of the long outer hairs with your fingers. If they pull out fairly easily you are ready to pluck. If not, wait a few more weeks and try again.

Begin plucking by brushing or combing the hair backwards, so it stands out from the dog's body. You can dust the coat with grooming powder or chalk to make it less slippery in your fingers. Hold the skin taut by pulling it with one hand. With the other hand, grasp a few hairs between your thumb and forefinger about an inch from the skin and pull them sharply in

*Grooming not only helps your dog stay attractive and healthy, but also is an enjoyable bonding experience.*

but can still be left somewhat longer than on the body. Make sure they have a smooth outline with no bumps over the pasterns. Finish by plucking the more delicate chest and anal regions, and use blunt-nosed scissors to carefully cut around the genitalia and foot edges. The finished JRT should have a neat outline to its body, but without the sculpted look seen in, for example, the Wire Fox Terrier. It should resemble a turned-out hunter rather than a caricature show dog. Nonetheless, preparation of the show dog's coat requires more than these basics and is best done the first time by an experienced JRT person.

Your JRT won't look her best until several weeks after being plucked, so don't put it off until the week before a dog event. After your dog's coat has grown back in, try to pluck just a little at a time so you can keep your dog looking her best without having another plucking marathon. Plucking should not be an ordeal. If it is, try doing less at one time, waiting for the hair to be more loosely attached, or even rethink how important it is for you to have your JRT looking perfect. In some cases, it may be kinder to resort to clipping.

**Bathing and Shampoos:** The proper harsh-coat texture can also be adversely affected by bathing, although special terrier shampoos are available that will soften the coat less. A show dog should be bathed about five to seven days before the show in order to avoid an overly soft coat. For the average well-kept JRT, there should be no need to bathe more than once every couple of months.

the direction of hair growth. You can also use a stripping comb to accomplish the job, which will save considerable finger fatigue. To use the stripping comb, place a few hairs between the comb and your thumb and pull in the direction of hair growth. Begin around the neck and shoulders and work backward and downward. The stripping comb can also be used to comb in the direction of hair growth when you are almost through to give the dog a final polished look. Plucking can irritate some dogs' skin, so you may wish to bathe your dog with an antibacterial or soothing shampoo when you finish.

The hair should be left slightly longer on the muzzle and chest. The legs should not be bottle-brush legs, as seen on many wire coated terriers,

Your JRT may have other ideas, and after she has perfumed herself with *eau de carrion*, you won't care about coat texture. A supply of rubber gloves comes in handy for such occasions. You will generally get better results with a shampoo made for dogs. Dog skin has a pH of 7.5, while human skin has a pH of 5.5; bathing in a shampoo formulated for the pH of human skin can lead to scaling and irritation in a dog. Most shampoos will kill fleas even if not especially formulated as a flea shampoo, but none has any residual killing action on fleas. No JRT owner should be without one of the shampoos that requires no water or rinsing. These are wonderful for puppies, spot-baths, emergencies, and bathing when time does not permit.

These are therapeutic shampoos for various skin problems:

✔ for dry scaly skin—moisturizing shampoos
✔ for excessive scale and dandruff—antiseborrheic shampoos
✔ for damaged skin—antimicrobials
✔ for itchy skin—oatmeal-based antipruritics

Use a handheld sprayer and hold the nozzle against the dog's skin and the dog will not be bothered as much as she would if the spray came from a distance. Use water of a temperature that would be comfortable for you to bathe in, and be sure to keep some running on your own hand in order to monitor any temperature changes. A fractious terrier could inadvertently hit a faucet knob and get scalded. If you keep one hand on your dog's neck or ear, she is less likely to splatter you with a wet dog shake.

*The groomed rough coat allows the lines of the body to show through, with a little extra left in the face for expression.*

Wet your dog down working forward from the rear. Once soaked, use your hand or a soft brush to work in the shampoo (it will go a lot further and be easier to apply if you first mix the shampoo with warm water. Rinse thoroughly, this time working from the head back. Don't use a cream rinse, which would soften the coat.

## Shedding

All coat types shed. Shedding is controlled not by exposure to warmer temperatures, but by exposure to longer periods of light. Thus, indoor dogs that are exposed to artificial light tend to shed somewhat all year.

*"Honest...we really tried to stay clean."*

For other grooming problems, note the following:

✔ Wet or muddy hair can be dried and cleaned by sprinkling on a liberal amount of cornstarch, rubbing it in, and brushing it out.

✔ Pine tar can be loosened with hair spray.

✔ Other tar can be worked out with vegetable oil followed by dishwashing detergent.

✔ Chewing gum can be eased out by first applying ice.

✔ For skunk odor, mix one pint of 3 percent hydrogen peroxide, ⅔ cup baking soda, and one teaspoon of liquid soap or citrus based dog shampoo with one gallon of water. Use immediately and leave it on the dog about five minutes; rinse and repeat.

## Beauty Is Skin Deep

Your JRT's good looks depend in part upon a healthy coat, but a healthy coat is impossible without healthy skin. Skin problems in all dogs are the most common problems seen by veteri-narians, and the most common of all skin problems is *flea allergy dermatitis (FAD).* Itchy, crusted bumps with hair loss in the region around the rump, especially at the base of the tail, results from a flea bite (actually, the flea's saliva) anywhere on the dog's body.

Besides FAD, dogs can have allergic reactions to pollens or other inhaled allergens. Allergies to weeds can manifest themselves between the dog's toes. Food allergies can also occur, but are uncommon.

*Pyoderma,* with pus-filled bumps and crusting, is another common skin disease. *Impetigo* is characterized by such bumps and crusting most often in the groin area of puppies. Both are treated with antibiotics and antibacterial shampoos.

A reddened moist itchy spot that suddenly appears is most likely a "hot spot," which arises from an itch-scratch-chew cycle resulting most commonly from fleas or flea allergy. Clip the surrounding hair, wash the area with an oat-meal-based shampoo, and prevent the dog from further chewing. Use an Elizabethan collar (available from your veterinarian or you can fashion one from a plastic pail), or an anti-chew preparation such as Bitter Apple (available from most pet stores). Your veterinarian can also prescribe anti-inflammatory medication.

In *seborrhea,* there may be excessive dandruff or greasiness, often with excessive ear wax and a rancid odor. Treatment is with anti-seborrheic shampoos or diet change.

Hair may be lost in a bilaterally symmetric pattern, without itching, due to hypothyroidism, Cushing's syndrome, or testicular tumors. Consult your veterinarian.

# Ticks, Fleas, and JRTs

## Ticks

Ticks can carry Rocky Mountain spotted fever, tick paralysis, Lyme disease, and most commonly, "tick fever" (ehrlichiosis), all potentially fatal diseases. They most often burrow in around the ears, head, neck, and feet. Use a tissue or tweezers to remove ticks, since some diseases can be transmitted to humans. Grasp the tick as close to the skin as possible, and pull slowly and steadily, trying not to leave the head in the dog. Clean the site with alcohol. Often a bump will remain after the tick is removed, even if you got the head. It will go away with time.

Two newer products for tick control are amitraz collars (tick collars) and fipronil spray or liquid. Neither will keep ticks totally off your dog, but they may discourage them from staying or implanting. Even with these precautions you should still use your hands to feel for ticks in your dogs whenever you are in a potential tick infested area.

## Fleas

Only a few years ago fighting fleas was a full time job and a losing battle. Recent advances have finally put dog owners on the winning side. In any but the mildest of infestations, the new products available are well worth their initial higher purchase price. It's a lot cheaper to put an expensive product on your dog once every three months than to reapply a cheap one every day.

Always read the ingredients. You may think you're getting a deal with a less expensive product that is applied the same and boasts of the same results as one of the more expensive products, but you're not getting a deal if it doesn't contain the right ingredients. Some of the major ingredients in the newer products are:

✔ imidacloprid (for example, Advantage) is a liquid applied once a month on the animal's back. It gradually distributes itself over the entire skin surface and kills at least 98 percent of the fleas on the animal within 24 hours and will continue to kill fleas for a month. It can withstand water, but not repeated swimming or bathing.

✔ fipronil (for example, Frontline) comes as either a spray that you must apply all over the dog's body or as a self-distributing liquid applied only on the dog's back. Once applied, fipronil collects in the hair follicles and then wicks out over time. Thus, it is resistant to being washed off and can kill fleas for up to three months on dogs. It is also effective on ticks for a shorter period.

✔ lufenuron (for example, Program) is given as a pill once a month. Fleas that bite the dog and ingest the lufenuron in the dog's system are rendered sterile. It is extremely safe. All animals in the environment must be treated in order for the regime to be effective, however.

Traditional flea control products are either less effective or less safe than these newer products. The permethrins and pyrethrins are safe, but have virtually no residual action. The large family of cholinesterase inhibitors (Dursban, Diazinon, malathion, Sevin, Carbaryl, ProSpot, Spotton) last a little longer, but have been known to kill dogs when overused, used in combination with cholinesterase inhibiting yard products, or with cholinesterase inhibiting dewormers. Ultrasonic flea repelling collars have been shown to be both ineffective on fleas and irritating to dogs. Feeding dogs brewer's yeast or garlic will not get rid of fleas.

## Tough as Nails

JRT nails were developed to withstand digging through and running over rocky terrain and hard-packed earth. Without this constant abrasion, they will grow overly long, causing discomfort, lameness, splayed feet, and painful split nails, and the toes will be more susceptible to injury. If dewclaws are left untrimmed, they can get caught on things more easily or actually loop around and grow into the dog's leg. You must prevent this by trimming your dog's nails every week or two.

Start young. Begin by handling the feet and nails daily, and then cutting the very tips of your puppy's nails every week, taking special care not to cut the "quick" (the central core of

*Freshly groomed and ready for a mud bath!*

blood vessels and nerve endings). You may find it easiest to cut the nails with your puppy lying on her back in your lap. With an adult, it is usually easier to hold the foot behind the dog, much like a blacksmith holds a horse's hoof. If you look at the bottoms of the nails you will see a solid core culminating in a hollowed nail. Cut the tip up to the core, but not beyond. On occasion you will slip up and cause the nail to bleed. This is best stopped by styptic powder or "shaving stick," but if this is not available dip the nail in flour, hold it to a wet tea bag, or drag it deep into a bar of soap.

*Cut the nails as close to the "quick" as possible.*

## Jack Plaque Attack

The accumulation of plaque and tartar is a major health problem in today's dogs. Dry food and hard dog biscuits, rawhide, and nylabone chewies are helpful, but not totally effective, at removing plaque. Brushing your JRT's teeth once or twice weekly (optimally, daily) with a child's toothbrush and special doggy toothpaste (available in pet stores or from your veterinarian) is the best plaque remover. If not removed, plaque will attract bacteria and minerals, which will harden into tartar. You may have to have your veterinarian clean your dog's teeth as often as once a year, more often in older dogs.

Neglected plaque and tartar can cause infections to form along the gum line. The infection can gradually work its way down the sides of the tooth until the entire root is undermined. The tissues and bone around the tooth erode, and the tooth finally falls out. Meanwhile, the bacteria may have entered the bloodstream and traveled throughout the body, causing infection in the kidneys and heart valves.

Between four and seven months of age, puppies will begin to shed their baby teeth and show off new permanent teeth. Often deciduous (baby) teeth, especially the canines (fangs), are not shed, so that the permanent tooth grows in beside the baby tooth. If this condition persists for over a week, consult your veterinarian. Retained baby teeth can cause misalignment of adult teeth.

*Brushing your dog's teeth will prevent costly dental procedures and disease. Left unattended, teeth can become seriously infected.*

## Be Ear Responsible

The dog's ear canal is made up of an initial long vertical segment that then abruptly angles to run horizontally toward the skull. This configuration provides a moist environment in which various ear infections can flourish. The semi-prick ear of the JRT allows adequate air circulation, thwarting many infections, but even JRTs can develop painful and serious ear problems.

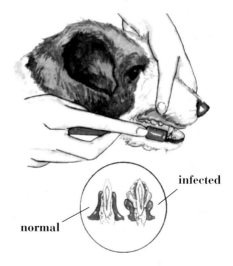

normal        infected

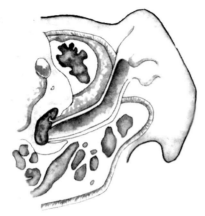

## Signs of Ear Problems

Inflammation, discharge, debris, foul odor, pain, scratching, shaking, tilting of the head, or circling to one side are all symptoms of ear problems. Extreme pain may indicate a ruptured eardrum. Bacterial and fungal infections, ear mites or ticks, foreign bodies, inhalant allergies, seborrhea, or hypothyroidism are

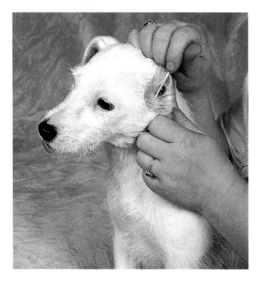

*The dog's ear canal consists of an initial vertical canal, with an abrupt curve leading to a horizontal canal.*

possible underlying problems. Grass awns are one of the most common causes of ear problems in dogs that spend time outdoors. Keep the ear lubricated with mineral oil, and seek veterinary treatment as soon as possible. Ear problems only get worse.

**Warning:** Don't use cotton swabs in the ear canal, as they can irritate the skin and pack debris into the horizontal canal. Never use powders in the ear, which can cake, or hydrogen peroxide, which leaves the ear moist.

## Ear Mites

Highly contagious and intensely irritating, ear mites are often found in puppies. Affected dogs will shake their head, scratch their ears, and carry their head sideways. A dark, dry, waxy buildup resembling coffee grounds in the ear canal, usually of both ears is the ear mite's signature. This material is actually dried blood mixed with ear wax. If you place some of this wax on a piece of dark paper, you may be able to see the tiny white moving culprits. Over-the-counter ear mite preparations can cause worse irritation. Ear mites are best treated by your veterinarian.

If you must treat the dog yourself, get a pyrethrin/mineral oil ear product. First flush the ear with an ear cleaning solution. You can buy a solution from your veterinarian, or make a mixture of one part alcohol to two parts white vinegar. Cleaning solutions will flush

*Accustom your dog to having its ears, eyes, mouth, and feet examined.*

debris but will not kill mites or cure infections. Apply the ear mite drops daily for at least a week, and possibly a month. Because these mites are also found in the dog's fur all over the body, you should also bathe the pet weekly with a pyrethrin based shampoo, or apply a pyrethrin flea dip, powder, or spray. Separate a dog with ear mites from other pets and wash your hands after handling the ears. Ideally, every pet in a household should be treated.

## The Smelly Dog

Doggy odor is not only offensive; it is unnatural. Don't exile the dog, or hold your breath. If a bath doesn't produce results, it's time to use your nose to pinpoint the source of the problem.

*All spiffed up and nowhere to go—he'll see about that!*

Infection is a common cause of bad odor; check the mouth, ears, feet, and genitals. Generalized bad odor can indicate a skin problem, such as seborrhea. Don't ignore bad odor, and don't make your dog take the blame for something you need to fix. Of course, sometimes it's simply the result of the dog's well-known penchant for rolling in the most foul-smelling substances available, in which case a bath is the cure!

JRT maintenance requires a little attention often, rather than a lot of attention seldom. A few minutes a day can help you stop a problem before it develops.

# JACK RUSSELL TERRIER MAINTENANCE AND REPAIR

Your dog can tell you where it hurts if you only know how to listen to her. You listen by means of a weekly health check and a regular veterinary checkup.

## The Health Check

A weekly health check should be part of your grooming procedure. The health check should include examining:

✔ the eyes for discharge, cloudiness, or discolored "whites"

✔ the ears for bad smell, redness, or discharge

✔ the mouth for red, bleeding, or swollen gums, loose teeth, ulcers of the tongue or gums, or bad breath

✔ the nose for thickened or colored discharge

✔ the skin for parasites, hair loss, crusts, red spots, or lumps

✔ the feet for cuts, abrasions, split nails, bumps, or misaligned toes.

Observe your dog for signs of lameness or incoordination, a sore neck, circling, loss of muscling, and for any behavioral change. Run your hands over the muscles and bones and check that they are symmetrical from one side to the other. Weigh your dog and observe whether she is putting on fat or wasting away. Check for any growths or swellings, which could be a sign of cancer or a number of less serious problems. A sore that does not heal, or any pigmented lump that begins to grow or bleed should be checked by a veterinarian immediately. Look out for mammary masses, changes in testicle size, discharge from the vulva or penis, increased or decreased urination, foul-smelling or strangely colored urine, incontinence, swollen abdomen, black or bloody stool, change in appetite or water consumption, difficulty breathing, lethargy, gagging, or loss of balance.

**To take your dog's temperature:** lubricate a rectal thermometer (preferably the digital type) and insert it about 1½ inches (3.8 cm), and leave it for about one minute. Do not allow your dog to sit down on the thermometer! Normal temperature for a JRT is around 101°F (38.3°C), ranging from 100 to 102.5°F (37.8°–39.2°C).

A good place to check the pulse is on the femoral artery, located inside the rear leg, where the thigh meets the abdomen. Normal pulse rates range from 80 to 100 beats per minute in an awake JRT, and are strong and fairly regular.

*Good health is the product of good care, good genes, and good luck.*

# The Health Team

Your health check can go only so far in ensuring your pet's healthy status. A good veterinarian will also be needed to monitor your dog's internal signs by way of blood tests and other procedures.

When choosing your veterinarian, consider availability, emergency arrangements, costs, facilities, and ability to communicate. Some veterinarians will include more sophisticated tests as part of their regular checkups, but such tests, while desirable, will add to the cost of a visit. Unless money is no object, reach an understanding about procedures and fees before having them performed. You and your veterinarian will form a team who will work together to protect your JRT's health, so your rapport with your veterinarian is very important. Your veterinarian should listen to your observations, and should explain to you exactly what is happening with your dog. The clinic should be clean, and have safe, sanitary overnight accommodations. After-hour emergency arrangements should be made clear.

When you take your JRT to the veterinary clinic, hold your dog on your lap or in a cage; don't let her bark, mingle with, or frighten other animals, who may be sick. If you think your dog may have a contagious illness, inform the clinic beforehand so that you can use another entrance. Your veterinarian will be appreciative if your JRT is clean, parasite-free, and under control during the examination. Warn your veterinarian if you think there is any chance that your dog may bite.

*The road to a long life begins at birth with good health care.*

*Internal organs of the Jack Russell Terrier.*

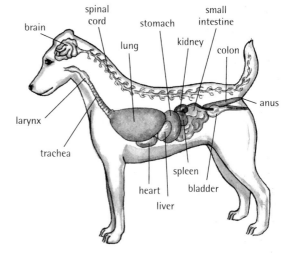

brain • spinal cord • stomach • small intestine • lung • kidney • colon • anus • larynx • trachea • spleen • heart • bladder • liver

# Emergencies

In general:

✔ Know the phone number and location of the emergency veterinarian in your area. In fact, write it on the top of this page or put it on your refrigerator.

✔ Always keep enough fuel in your car to make it to the emergency clinic without having to stop to find a gas station.

✔ Make sure breathing passages are open. Remove any collar and check the mouth and throat.

✔ Be calm and reassuring. A calm dog is less likely to go into shock.

✔ Move the dog as little and as gently as possible.

✔ Control any bleeding.

✔ Check airway, breathing, and circulation.

✔ Check for signs of shock (very pale gums, weakness, unresponsiveness, faint pulse, shivering). Treat by keeping the dog warm and calm.

✔ Never use force or do anything that causes extreme discomfort.

✔ Never remove an impaled object (unless it is blocking the airway).

## Electrical Shock

**Signs:** Collapse, burns inside mouth.

**Treatment:** Before touching the dog, disconnect plug or cut power; if that cannot be done immediately, use a wooden pencil, spoon, or broom handle to knock cord away from dog. Keep the dog warm and treat for shock. Monitor breathing and heartbeat.

## Poisonous Snakebites

**Signs:** Swelling, discoloration, pain, fangmarks, restlessness, nausea, weakness.

**Treatment:** Restrain the dog and keep him quiet. Only if you can't get to the veterinarian, apply a pressure bandage between the bite and the heart, tight enough to prevent blood from returning to the heart. For dogs bitten on the muzzle, a pressure bandage is not feasible. Never use a tourniquet.

## Deep Burns

**Signs:** Charred or pearly white skin; deeper layers of tissue exposed.

**Treatment:** Cool the burned area with cool packs, towels soaked in ice water, or by immersing in cold water. If over 50 percent of the dog is burned, do not immerse as this may cause shock. Cover the area with clean bandage or towel to avoid contamination. Do not apply pressure; do not apply ointments. Monitor for shock.

*Know your plants! Don't let poisonous plants tempt your dog.*

## Severe Allergic Reaction

Insect stings are the most common cause of extreme reactions. Swelling around the nose and throat can block the airway. Other signs are restlessness, vomiting, diarrhea, seizures, and collapse. These symptoms indicate an emergency; call the veterinarian immediately.

## Inability to Urinate

Blockage of urine can result in death. Inability to urinate is an emergency; call the veterinarian immediately.

## Poisoning

Symptoms and treatment vary depending upon the specific poison. If possible, bring the poison and its container with you. If in doubt about whether poison was ingested, call the veterinarian anyway. The most common and life-threatening poison eaten by dogs is ethylene glycol (antifreeze). Veterinary treatment must be obtained within two to four hours of ingestion of even tiny amounts if the dog's life is to be saved.

Rodent and insect baits also attract dogs and require immediate veterinary attention.

**Signs:** Vary according to poison, but commonly include vomiting, convulsions, staggering, or collapse.

**Treatment:** Call the veterinarian or poison control hotline and give as much information as possible. You may need to induce vomiting (except in the cases outlined below) by giving either hydrogen peroxide (mixed 1:1 with water), salt water, or dry mustard and water. Treat for shock and get to the veterinar-

## Other Potential Emergencies

In the following situations, *administer first aid*, then call your veterinarian to see if your dog should be seen on an emergency basis. This will depend upon the severity and extensiveness of the problem.

**Animal bites:** Allow some bleeding. Clean the area thoroughly. Antibiotic therapy will probably be necessary.

**Insect stings:** Remove any visible stingers. Administer baking soda and water paste to bee stings, and vinegar to wasp stings. Clean the area and apply antibacterial ointment. Monitor for allergic reaction.

Situations not described in this list can usually be treated with the same first aid as for humans. *In all cases, the best advice is to seek the opinion of a veterinarian.*

ian at once. Be prepared for convulsions or respiratory distress.

*Do not induce vomiting* if the poison was an acid, alkali, petroleum product, solvent, cleaner, tranquilizer, or if a sharp object was swallowed; also do not induce vomiting if the dog is severely depressed, convulsing, comatose, or if over two hours have passed since ingestion. If the dog is not convulsing or unconscious dilute the poison by giving milk, vegetable oil, or egg whites. Activated charcoal can adsorb many toxins. Baking soda or milk of magnesia can be given for ingested acids, and vinegar or lemon juice for ingested alkalis.

# The First Aid/Medical Kit

You should maintain a first aid/medical kit for your Jack Russell, which should contain:
✔ rectal thermometer
✔ scissors
✔ tweezer
✔ sterile gauze dressings
✔ self-adhesive bandage
✔ instant cold compress
✔ antidiarrhea medication (Immodium or prescription medication from your veterinarian)
✔ ophthalmic ointment (from your veterinarian)
✔ soap
✔ antiseptic skin ointment (from your veterinarian)
✔ hydrogen peroxide
✔ clean sponge
✔ pen light
✔ syringe
✔ towel
✔ first aid instructions
✔ veterinarian and emergency clinic numbers
✔ poison control center number.

# Preventive Medicine

The best preventive medicine is that which prevents accidents: a well-trained dog in a securely fenced yard or on a leash, and a properly terrier-proofed home. However, other preventive steps must be taken to avoid diseases and parasites.

## Medications

When giving pills, open your dog's mouth and place the pill well to the back and in the middle of the tongue. Close the mouth and gently stroke the throat until your dog swallows. Pre-wetting capsules or, better, covering them with cream cheese or some similar food, helps prevent capsules from sticking to the tongue or roof of the mouth. For liquid medicine, tilt the head back and place the liquid in the pouch of the cheek. Then close your dog's mouth until she swallows. Always give the full course of medications prescribed by your veterinarian. Don't give your dog human medications unless you have been directed to do so by your veterinarian as some medications for humans have no effect upon dogs, and some can have a very detrimental effect.

## Vaccinations

Vaccinations are available for several diseases. Some vaccinations are mandatory from a legal standpoint, some mandatory from a good sense standpoint, and some optional. Recent studies have implicated repeated vaccinations with combinations of vaccines with some autoimmune problems, in which the immune system turns against parts of the body. Some veterinarians thus recommend staggering different types of vaccines, and discourage over-vaccination. They also discourage vaccination in any dog that is under stress or not feeling well. Many dogs seem to feel under the weather for a day or so after getting their vaccinations, so don't schedule your appointment the day before boarding, a trip, or a big doggy event.

Several respected veterinary teaching hospitals have recently revised their vaccination protocols to include fewer booster shots. One such protocol suggests giving a three shot series for puppies, each shot containing parvovirus, adenovirus 2 (CAV-2), parainfluenza (CPIV), and distemper, with one rabies vaccination at 16 weeks. Following this a booster is given one year later, and then subsequent boosters are given every three years. They also recommend vaccinating for Lyme disease or leptospirosis only in endemic areas. Other respected epidemiologists disagree and prefer the traditional vaccination schedule. Confer with your veterinarian about current thinking on the matter. One thing is for sure: no matter what their possible side effects, vaccinations are a good thing, and all dogs must be vaccinated for their health as well as the health of others.

Puppies receive their dam's immunity through nursing in the first days of life. This is why it is important that your pup's mother be properly immunized before breeding, and that your pup be able to nurse from its dam. The immunity gained from the mother will wear off after several weeks, and then the pup will be susceptible to disease unless you provide immunity through vaccinations. The problem is that there is no way to know exactly when this passive immunity will wear off, and vaccinations given before that time are ineffective. So you must revaccinate over a period of weeks so that your pup will not be unprotected and will receive lasting immunity.

Your pup's breeder will have given the first vaccinations to your pup before it was old enough to go home with you. Bring all information about your pup's vaccination history to your veterinarian on your first visit so that the pup's vaccination schedule can be maintained. Meanwhile, it is best not to let your pup mingle with strange dogs.

# Internal Parasite Control

**Heartworms:** Heartworms are a deadly nematode parasite carried by mosquitoes; therefore, wherever mosquitoes are present, dogs should be on heartworm prevention. Several effective types of heartworm preventive are available, with some also preventing

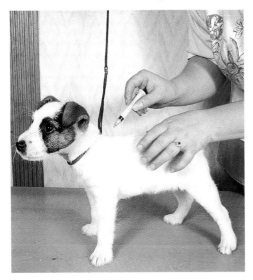

*Vaccinations are essential, but understand the vaccinations your dog receives and discuss their necessity with your veterinarian.*

# TIP

## Why You Don't Want to Breed Your JRT

Before you proceed with plans to breed your JRT, consider the following:

✔ There are many more Jack Russell Terriers born than there are good homes for them; therefore, the puppy you sell to a less than perfect buyer may end up neglected, abused, or discarded.

✔ The fact that your JRT is purebred and registered does not mean it is breeding quality, any more than the fact that you have a driver's license qualifies you to build race cars. Review the definition of breeding quality on page 28.

✔ JRTs typically have from five to seven puppies. Breeding so you can keep only one puppy ignores the fact that six others may not get a good home.

✔ Selling a litter will probably not come close to reimbursing you for the stud fee, prenatal care, possible whelping complications, Caesarean sections, supplemental feeding, puppy food, vaccinations, advertising, and a staggering investment of time and energy.

✔ Responsible breeders have spent years researching genetics and the breed, breed only the best specimens, and screen for hereditary defects in order to obtain superior puppies. Until you have done the same, you are undoing the hard work of those who have dedicated their lives to bettering the breed.

✔ There is definite discomfort and some danger when whelping a litter. Watching a litter being born is *not* a good way to teach the children the miracle of life—there are too many things that can go wrong.

✔ A spayed female is much less likely to develop breast cancer and a number of other hormone-related diseases. She should be spayed before her first season in order to avoid these problems.

---

many other types of worms. Ask your veterinarian when your puppy should begin taking the preventive. If you forget to give it as prescribed, your dog may get heartworms. A dog with suspected heartworms should not be given the daily preventive because a fatal reaction could occur. Heartworms are treatable in their early stages, but the treatment is expensive and not without risks (although a less risky treatment has recently become available). If untreated, heartworms can kill your pet.

**Intestinal parasites:** Hookworms, whipworms, ascarids, threadworms, and lungworms are all types of nematode parasites that can infect dogs of all ages, but have their most devastating effect on puppies. When you take the pup to be vaccinated, bring along a stool specimen so that your veterinarian can also check for these parasites. Most puppies do have worms at some point, even pups from the most fastidious breeders. This is because some types of larval worms become encysted in the

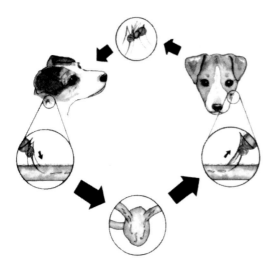

*The life cycle of heartworms. When a mosquito bites an infected dog, it ingests circulating immature heartworms, which it then passes on to the next dog it bites.*

because fleas transmit tapeworms to dogs. Some tapeworms can also be contracted from rodent, deer, and rabbit carcasses. Tapeworms look like moving white worms on fresh stools, or may dry up and look like rice grains around the dog's anus. Tapeworms are one of the least harmful worms, but their segments can be irritating to the dog's anal region, and are certainly unsightly.

## Common Misconceptions About Worms

✔ **Misconception:** A dog that is "scooting" its rear along the ground has worms. Although this may be a sign of tapeworms, a dog that repeatedly scoots more likely has impacted anal sacs.

✔ **Misconception:** Feeding a dog sugar and sweets will give it worms. There are good reasons not to feed a dog sweets, but worms have nothing to do with them.

✔ **Misconception:** Dogs should be regularly wormed every month or so. Dogs should be wormed when, and only when, they have been diagnosed with worms. No worm medication is completely without risk, and it is foolish to use it carelessly.

**Protozoa:** Puppies and dogs also suffer from protozoan parasites, such as coccidia and especially, *Giardia*. These can cause chronic or intermittent diarrhea, and can be diagnosed with a stool specimen.

dam's body long before she ever became pregnant, perhaps when she herself was a pup. Here they lie dormant and immune from worming, until hormonal changes due to her pregnancy cause them to be activated, and then they infect her fetuses or her newborns through her milk. You may be tempted to pick up some worm medication and worm your puppy yourself. Don't. Over-the-counter wormers are largely ineffective and often more dangerous than those available through your veterinarian. Left untreated, worms can cause vomiting, diarrhea, dull coat, listlessness, anemia, and death. Have your puppy tested for internal parasites regularly. Some heartworm preventives also prevent most types of intestinal worms (but not tapeworms).

**Tapeworms** (cestodes) tend to plague some dogs throughout their lives. There is no preventive, except to diligently rid your JRT of fleas,

# Common Ailments and Symptoms

## Coughing

Allergies, foreign bodies, pneumonia, tracheal collapse, tumors, and especially kennel cough and heart disease, can all cause coughing.

**Kennel cough** is a highly communicable airborne disease caused by several different infectious agents, but all cause similar symptoms. It is characterized by a gagging cough arising eight days after exposure. Inoculations are available and are an especially good idea if you plan to have your dog around other dogs at training classes or while being boarded.

**Heart disease** can result in coughing, most often in older dogs following exercise or in the evening. The dog will often lie down with her head pointed upward. Treatment with diuretics prescribed by your veterinarian can help alleviate the coughing for a while.

Any persistent cough should be checked by your veterinarian. Coughing irritates the throat and can lead to secondary infections if allowed to continue unchecked. It can also be miserable for the dog.

## Vomiting

Vomiting is a common occurrence that may or may not indicate a serious problem. Vomiting after eating grass is common and usually of no great concern. Overeating is a common cause of occasional vomiting in puppies, especially if they follow eating with playing. Feed smaller meals more frequently if this becomes a problem. Vomiting immediately after meals could indicate an obstruction of the esophagus. Repeated vomiting could indicate that the dog has eaten spoiled food, undigestible objects, or may have a stomach illness. Veterinary advice should be sought. Meanwhile, withhold food (or feed as directed for diarrhea) and restrict water.

Consult your veterinarian immediately if your dog vomits a foul substance resembling fecal matter (indicating a blockage in the intestinal tract), blood (partially digested blood resembles coffee grounds), or if there is projectile or continued vomiting. Sporadic vomiting with poor appetite and generally poor condition could indicate internal parasites or a more serious internal disease that should also be checked by your veterinarian.

## Diarrhea

Diarrhea can result from overexcitement or nervousness, a change in diet or water, sensitivity to certain foods, overeating, intestinal parasites, viral or bacterial infections, or ingestion of toxic substances. Bloody diarrhea, diarrhea with vomiting, fever, or other signs of toxicity, or diarrhea that lasts for more than a day should not be allowed to continue without veterinary advice. Some of these could be symptomatic of potentially fatal disorders.

Less severe diarrhea can be treated at home by withholding or severely restricting food and water for 24 hours. Ice cubes can be given to satisfy thirst. Administer Immodium in the same weight dosage as recommended for humans. A bland diet consisting of rice, tapioca, or cooked macaroni, along with cottage cheese or tofu for protein, should be given for several days. Feed nothing else. The intestinal tract needs time off in order to heal.

## Urinary Tract Diseases

If your dog has difficulty or pain in urination, urinates suddenly and often but in small amounts, or passes cloudy or bloody urine, he may be suffering from a problem of the bladder, urethra, or prostate.

In males, infections of the *prostate gland* can lead to repeated urinary tract infections, and sometimes painful defecation or blood and pus in the urine. Castration and long-term antibiotic therapy is required for improvement.

Dribbling of urine during sleep indicates a hormonal problem. Urinalysis and a rectal exam by your veterinarian are necessary to diagnose the exact nature of the problem. Bladder infections must be treated promptly to prevent the infection from reaching the kidneys.

**Kidney disease,** ultimately leading to kidney failure, is one of the most common ailments of older dogs. The earliest symptom is usually increased urination. Although the excessive urination may cause problems in keeping your house clean or your night's sleep intact, *never* try to restrict water from a dog with kidney disease. Increased urination can also be a sign of diabetes or a urinary tract infection. Your veterinarian can discover the cause with some simple tests, and each of these conditions can be treated. For kidney disease, a diet low in phosphorus and, often, protein is prescribed.

## Impacted Anal Sacs

Constant licking of the anus or scooting along the ground are characteristic signs of anal sac impaction. Dogs have two anal sacs that are normally emptied by rectal pressure during defecation. Their musky smelling contents may also be forcibly ejected when a dog is extremely frightened. Sometimes they fail to empty properly and become impacted or infected. This is more common in small dogs, obese dogs, dogs with seborrhea, and dogs that seldom have firm stools. Impacted sacs cause extreme discomfort and can become infected. Treatment consists of manually emptying the sacs and administering antibiotics. As a last resort, the sacs may be removed surgically.

## Endocrine Disorders

The most widespread hormone related disorders in dogs are diabetes, hypothyroidism, and Cushing's syndrome. The hallmark of diabetes is increased drinking and urination and sometimes an increased appetite with weight loss. It is most common in obese spayed females. Diabetes can be diagnosed with a simple test, and treatment is available.

**Hypothyroidism,** the most common of these, also has the least obvious symptoms, which may include weight gain, lethargy, and coat problems such as oiliness, dullness, symmetrical hair loss, and hair that is easily pulled out. The simplest test for hypothyroidism is a blood test for baseline serum T4 level. This test, however, is only recommended for identifying dogs with normal thyroid function; it should never be used as the final test to diagnose abnormal thyroid function. More definitive tests include free T4 measured by equilibrium dialysis (fT4ed) and canine thyroid stimulating hormone (cTSH) measurements. Treatment for hypothyroidism is with daily medication, and progress monitored with retesting in about two months.

**Cushing's syndrome** (hyperadrenocorticism) is seen mostly in older dogs, and is characterized by increased drinking and urination, a pot-bellied appearance, symmetrical hair loss on the body, darkened skin, and susceptibility to

*The face of good health is free of discharges and filled with enthusiasm.*

infections. This condition can be diagnosed and treated by your veterinarian.

## Cancers

As in humans, cancer is a major threat in dogs. Mammary gland tumors are among the most common cancers in the dog, occurring mostly in females that were not spayed early in life. Spaying after the age of two years doesn't impart the protection from mammary cancer that earlier spaying does. Approximately 50 percent of all mammary tumors are malignant.

Lymphosarcoma is another of the more commonly seen cancers in dogs. It affects the blood and lymph systems; symptoms may include swelling of the lymph nodes, especially those of the lower neck area and behind the "knees." Chemotherapy can extend the life of many affected dogs.

## Eye Problems

A watery discharge can be a symptom of a foreign body, allergies, corneal ulcer, or a tear drainage problem. If accompanied by squinting or pawing at the eye, suspect a foreign body in it. Examine under the lids and flood the eye with saline solution, or use a moist cotton swab to remove any debris. A clogged tear drainage duct can cause the tears to drain onto the face, rather than the normal drainage through the nose. Your veterinarian can diagnose a drainage problem with a simple test.

**KCS:** A thick ropey mucous or crusty discharge suggests conjunctivitis or dry eye (*keratoconjunctivitis sicca*, or KCS). In KCS there is inadequate tear production, resulting in irritation

to the surface of the eye whenever the dog blinks. The surface of the eye may appear dull. KCS can cause secondary bacterial infection or corneal ulcers. In fact, KCS should be suspected in any dog in which recurrent corneal ulceration or conjunctivitis is a problem. In past years, treatment of KCS was with the frequent application of artificial tears, which most owners found difficult to perform as often as needed. Recent drug advances treat KCS with ophthalmic immunosuppressive therapy. This therapy can be quite effective if begun early.

**Cataracts:** As your JRT ages it's natural that the lens of the eye becomes a little hazy. You will notice this as a slightly grayish appearance behind the pupils. But if this occurs at a young age, or if the lens looks white or opaque, ask your veterinarian to check your dog for cataracts. In cataracts the lens becomes so opaque that light can no longer reach the retina. As in humans, the lens can be surgically removed. It can also be replaced with an artificial lens, but most dogs seem to do well without replacement.

**Lens luxation** is an inherited disorder in Jack Russells and many other terriers. The lens is normally held in place behind the iris by a ring of thin fibers (called zonules), but if these attachments are lost the lens will float out of position, sometimes even protruding through the pupil. A totally displaced ("luxated") lens is painful; the eye will be red and possibly opaque. If vision is to be saved, the lens must be removed immediately. A partially displaced ("subluxated") lens has less obvious symptoms, and may be treated medically. In some cases you can see the edge of the lens through the pupil, or the lens may even fall through the pupillary opening so that it is partially in front of the iris. Dogs with either condition, unless obviously arising from trauma, should not be bred. Lens luxation is also discussed on page 15.

Any time your dog's pupils do not constrict in response to light, or when one eye reacts differently from another, take the dog to the veterinarian immediately. It could indicate a serious ocular or neurological problem.

## Limping

Limping may or may not indicate a serious problem. Mild lameness should be treated by complete rest; if it still persists after three days, your dog will need to be examined by the veterinarian. When associated with extreme pain, fever, swelling, deformity, or grinding or popping sounds, you should have your veterinarian examine your JRT at once. Ice packs may help minimize swelling if applied immediately after an injury.

**Knee injuries,** especially ruptured cruciate ligaments, are common in dogs; most do not get well on their own. Avoid pain medications that might encourage the use of an injured limb. Luxating patellas (see page 15) are also a problem in many dogs and may need surgical correction. Affected dogs will usually hold up a rear leg every few steps.

Puppies are especially susceptible to bone and joint injuries, and should never be allowed to jump from high places or run until exhausted. Persistent limping in puppies may result from one of several developmental bone problems, and should be checked by the veterinarian. Both puppies and adults should be kept from playing and running on slippery floors that could cause them to lose their footing.

**Arthritis:** In older dogs, or dogs with a previous injury, limping is often the result of osteoarthritis. In some dogs there is no obvious cause. In others, abnormal stresses or trauma to the joint can cause degeneration of the joint cartilage and underlying bone and

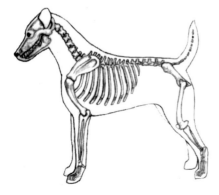

*The Jack Russell Terrier skeleton.*

inflame the surrounding membrane. The bone develops small bony outgrowths, which along with the other changes, cause the joint to stiffen, become painful, and have a decreased range of motion.

Conservative treatment entails keeping the dog's weight down, attending to injuries, and maintaining a program of exercise. Low impact exercise, such as walking or swimming every other day, is best for dogs with signs of arthritis. Newer drugs, such as carprofen, are available from your veterinarian and may help alleviate some of the symptoms, but they should be used only with careful veterinary supervision. Some newer drugs and supplements may actually improve the joint. Polysulfated glycosaminoglycan increases the compressive resilience of cartilage. Glucosamine stimulates the synthesis of collagen, and may help rejuvenate cartilage to some extent. Chondroitin sulfate helps to shield cartilage from destructive enzymes.

Also see discussion of skin, ear, and dental problems, pages 78–81.

# The Old Friend

The spry JRT ages well and lives long. Eventually, though, you will notice that your dog sleeps longer and more soundly than she did as a youngster. Upon awakening, she is slower to get going and may be stiff at first. She may be less eager to play and more content to lie in the sun. She may even become obedient!

Both physical activity and metabolic rates decrease in older animals, meaning that they require fewer calories to maintain the same weight. It is important to keep your older dog active. Older dogs that are fed the same as when they were young risk becoming obese; they have a greater risk of cardiovascular and joint problems, and metabolic diseases.

Older dogs should be fed several small meals instead of one large meal, and should be fed on time. Moistening dry food or feeding canned food can help a dog with dental problems enjoy her meal.

Although many geriatric dogs are overweight, others lose weight and may need to eat a special diet in order to keep the pounds on. Most older dogs do not require a special diet unless they have a particular medical need for it (such as obesity: low calorie; kidney failure: low protein; heart failure: low sodium).

**Odors:** Older dogs tend to have a stronger body odor, but you shouldn't just ignore increased odors. They could indicate specific problems, such as periodontal disease, impacted anal sacs, seborrhea, ear infections, or even kidney disease. Any strong odor should be checked by your veterinarian. Like people, dogs lose skin moisture as they age, and though dogs don't have to worry about wrinkles, their skin can become dry and itchy. Regular brushing can help by stimulating oil production.

**Immune system:** The immune system may be less effective in older dogs, so it is increasingly important to shield your dog from infectious disease, chilling, overheating, and any stressful conditions.

**Anesthesia risk:** Older dogs present a somewhat greater anesthesia risk. Most of this increased risk can be negated, however, by first screening dogs with a complete medical workup.

**Vomiting and diarrhea** in an old dog can signal many different problems. Keep in

some dogs, especially those with diabetes, may develop cataracts. These can be removed by a veterinary ophthalmologist if they are severe. Decreased tear production increases the chances of KCS (dry eye) (see page 95). Dogs with gradual vision loss can cope well as long as they are kept in familiar surroundings, and extra safety precautions are followed.

Long trips may be grueling, and boarding in a kennel may be extremely upsetting. Introduction of a puppy or new pet may be welcomed and encourage your older dog to play, but if your dog is not used to other dogs the newcomer will more likely be resented and be an additional source of stress.

In general, any ailment that an older dog has is magnified in severity compared to the same symptoms in a younger dog. Don't be lulled into a false sense of security just because you own a Jack Russell Terrier and they are usually known to live long lives. A long life depends upon good genes, good care, and good luck.

If you are lucky enough to have an old JRT, you still must accept that an end will come. Heart disease, kidney failure, and cancer eventually claim most of these senior citizens. Early detection can help delay their effects, but unfortunately, can seldom prevent them ultimately.

mind that a small older dog cannot tolerate the dehydration that results from continued vomiting or diarrhea and you should not let it continue unchecked. The older dog should be seen by her veterinarian at least twice a year. Blood tests can detect early stages of diseases that can benefit from treatment.

Some older dogs become cranky and less patient, especially when dealing with puppies or boisterous children. But don't just excuse behavioral changes, especially if sudden, as due simply to aging. They could be symptoms of pain or disease.

**Impaired senses:** Older dogs may experience hearing or visual loss. Be careful not to startle a dog with impaired senses, as a startled dog could snap in self-defense. The slight haziness that appears in the older dog's pupils is normal and has minimal effect upon vision, but

# Saying Farewell

Jack Russell Terriers live a long time, but they do not live forever. Despite the best of care, a time will come when neither you nor your veterinarian can prevent your cherished pet from succumbing to old age or an incurable illness. It seems hard to believe that you will have to say good-bye to one who has been such a focal point of your life—in truth, a real member of your family. That dogs live such a short time compared to humans is a cruel fact, but one that all owners must ultimately face.

You should realize that both of you have been fortunate to have shared so many good times, but make sure that your JRT's remaining time is still pleasurable. Many terminal illnesses make your dog very ill indeed, and there comes a point where your desire to keep your friend with you as long as possible may not be the kindest thing for either of you. If your dog no longer eats her dinner or treats, it is a sign that she doesn't feel well and you must face the prospect of doing what is best for your beloved friend.

## Euthanasia

Euthanasia is a difficult and personal decision that no one wishes to make, and no one can make for you. Ask your veterinarian if there is a reasonable chance of your dog getting better, and if it is likely that your dog is suffering. Ask yourself if your dog is getting pleasure out of life, and if she enjoys most of her days. Financial considerations can be a factor if it means going into debt in exchange for just a little while longer. Your own emotional state must also be considered.

If you do decide that euthanasia is the kindest farewell gift for your beloved friend, discuss with your veterinarian beforehand what will happen. Euthanasia is painless and involves giving an overdose of an anesthetic. If your dog is fearful of the veterinarian clinic, you might feel better having the doctor meet you at home or come out to your car. Although it won't be easy, try to remain with your dog so that her last

moments will be filled with your love; otherwise, have a friend your Jack Russell knows stay with her. Try to recall the wonderful times you have shared and realize that, however painful losing such a once-in-a-lifetime dog is, it is better than never having had such a partner at all.

Many people who regarded their JRT as a member of the family nonetheless feel embarrassed at the grief they feel at her loss. Yet this dog has often functioned as a surrogate child, best friend, and confidant. Partnership with a pet can be one of the closest and most stable relationships in many people's lives. Because people are often closer to their pets than they are to distant family members, it is not uncommon to feel more grief at the loss of the pet. Unfortunately, the support from friends that comes with human loss is too often absent with pet loss. Such well-meaning but ill-informed statements as "he was just a dog" or "just get another one" do little to ease the pain, but the truth is that many people simply don't know how to react and probably aren't really as callous as they might sound. There are, however, many people who share your feelings and there are pet bereavement counselors available at many veterinary schools.

After losing such a cherished friend, many people say they will never get another dog. True, no dog will ever take the place of your dog. But you will find that another JRT is a welcome diversion and will help keep you from dwelling on the loss of your first pet, as long as you don't keep comparing the new dog to the old. True also, by getting another Jack Russell you are sentencing yourself to the same grief in another 10 to 15 years, but wouldn't you rather have that than miss out on a second once-in-a-lifetime dog?

For the following emergencies there may be no time to seek veterinary guidance. *Initiate first aid; then transport to the veterinarian immediately (call first).*

**Breathing Difficulties**

**Signs:** Gasping for breath with head extended, anxiety, weakness; advances to loss of consciousness, bluish tongue (Exception: Carbon monoxide poisoning causes bright red tongue).

**Treatment:** If not breathing, give mouth-to-nose resuscitation:

**1.** Open the dog's mouth, clear passage of secretions and foreign bodies.

**2.** Pull the tongue forward.

**3.** Seal your mouth over the dog's nose and mouth, blow gently into the dog's nose for three seconds, then release.

**4.** Continue until the dog breathes on his own.

If due to **drowning,** turn the dog upside down, holding him by the hind legs, so that water can run out of his mouth. Then administer mouth-to-nose resuscitation, with the dog's head positioned lower than his lungs.

For **obstructions,** wrap your hands around the abdomen, behind the rib cage, and compress briskly. Repeat if needed. If the dog loses consciousness, extend the head and neck forward, pull the tongue out fully, and explore the throat for any foreign objects.

**Shock**

**Signs:** Very pale gums, weakness, unresponsiveness, faint pulse, shivering.

**Treatment:** Keep the dog warm and calm; control any bleeding; check breathing, pulse, and consciousness and treat these problems if needed.

**Heatstroke**

**Signs:** Rapid, loud breathing; abundant thick saliva, bright red mucous membranes, high rectal temperature. **Later signs:** Unsteadiness, diarrhea, coma.

**Treatment:** Cover the dog with a cold wet towel and place him in front of a fan. If this is not possible, immerse the dog in cool water. *Do not plunge the dog in ice water.* Offer small amounts of water for drinking. You must lower your dog's body temperature quickly (but do not lower it below 100°F [37.8°C]).

**Hypothermia**

**Signs:** Shivering, cold feeling, sluggishness.

**Treatment:** Warm gradually. Wrap the dog in a blanket. Place plastic bottles filled with hot water outside the blankets

*Cool a dog with heatstroke by covering him with wet towels and placing him in front of a fan. Dunking the dog in ice water is dangerous because it constricts peripheral blood vessels.*

(not touching the dog). You can also place a plastic wrap over the blanket, making sure the dog's head is not covered. Don't use heat lamps, which too often result in burns or excessive heating. Monitor temperature with thermometer.

## Convulsions or Seizures

**Signs:** Drooling, stiffness, muscle spasms.

**Treatment:** Wrap the dog securely in a blanket to prevent him from injuring himself on furniture or stairs. Remove other dogs from the area (they may attack the convulsing dog). Never put your hands (or anything) in a convulsing dog's mouth. Monitor for shock. Make note of all characteristics and sequences of seizure activity, which can help to diagnose the cause.

## Eye Injuries

For contact with irritants, flush for five minutes with water or saline solution. For injuries, cover with clean gauze soaked in water or saline solution.

## Hypoglycemia (Low Blood Sugar)

**Signs:** The dog appears disoriented, weak, staggering. He may appear blind, and the muscles may twitch. Later stages lead to convulsions, coma, and death. Most often seen in small dogs, or dogs that have been very active and have not been fed.

**Treatment:** Give food, or honey or syrup mixed with warm water.

## Open Wounds

**Signs:** Consider wounds to be an emergency if there is profuse bleeding, if extremely deep, if open to chest cavity, abdominal cavity, or head.

**Treatment:** Control massive bleeding first. Cover the wound with clean dressing and apply pressure; apply more dressings over the others

*Apply pressure to the closest pressure point for uncontrolled bleeding of an extremity.*

until bleeding stops. Also elevate the wound site, and apply cold pack to site. If an extremity, apply pressure to the closest pressure point as follows:

✔ for a front leg—inside of front leg just above the elbow

✔ for a rear leg—inside of thigh where the femoral artery crosses the thigh bone

✔ for the tail—underside of tail close to where it joins the body

Use a tourniquet only in life-threatening situations and when all other attempts have failed. Check for signs of shock.

**Sucking chest wounds:** Place sheet of plastic or other nonporous material over the hole and bandage it to make as air-tight a seal as possible.

**Abdominal wounds:** Place warm, wet, sterile dressing over any protruding internal organs; cover with bandage or towel. Do not attempt to push organs back into the dog.

**Head wounds:** Apply gentle pressure to control bleeding. Monitor for loss of consciousness or shock and treat accordingly.

## A Walk on the Wild Side

JRTs can entertain themselves quite ably within the confines of your own yard, but some of that entertainment may include digging up your garden, ripping down hanging clothes, and gnawing on your house. Regular exercise will lessen this misdirected energy considerably.

### JRTs in the Great Outdoors

JRTs are equally adept at finding trouble afield. You will find your visions of a faithful dog trotting by your side at odds with the JRT's instinctive urge to root out some vermin. Bringing along another reliable dog that stays with you is the best training aid you can have; otherwise, staying in an area with defined paths and walking along them at a brisk pace seems to work better than simply standing in the middle of a field or the woods. The chance of your dog wandering off to hunt is less if you avoid thick wooded areas or any areas chock full of game. JRTs won't hesitate to give chase to any size game, and it is your responsibility to know your running area thoroughly before ever removing your JRT's leash. Explore an area with your JRT on a long lead several times before trusting him off lead.

If you want to trust your JRT, trust him first in an enclosed area such as a fenced ball field or empty schoolyard. Bring some treats so you

*Jack Russells are always on the lookout for the next challenge.*

can practice off-lead recalls. You may even want to make sure that your dog is already hungry (and maybe a little tired) beforehand. When your dog comes, praise him, hand him a treat, then let him go again so he doesn't associate coming with relinquishing his freedom.

### The JRT Off Lead

When your dog is returning to you reliably in a fenced area, you may wish to venture farther afield. Note that walking a JRT off lead entails some risk, which you should carefully consider before you unsnap the leash. One of the deadliest killers of JRTs is trust. The JRT is not a retriever that can be trusted to walk off lead by your side down a country road, or to sit in your unfenced front yard. As trustworthy as your JRT may be, he can't help but follow his instinct to answer the call of the wild and to chase game, and far too often he's off like a bolt after a cat in the distance, across the path of an oncoming vehicle.

In many areas there simply are no safe places in which to run your terrier off lead. Your dog can get ample exercise and enjoyment from a walk on lead. Before walking on lead, double check that your dog's collar cannot slip over his head. A startled dog can frantically back out of his collar unless it is snug. Once he learns this little trick, he won't hesitate to employ it to get a closer look at the neighbor's cats along the route. If you use a retractable leash, never allow so much loose lead that your dog could suddenly jump in the path of a passing vehicle. Be

prepared for the typical Jack Russell jackrabbit starts and jackknife turns.

If you pick a regular time of day for your walk, you will have your own personal fitness coach goading you off the couch like clockwork. Check your dog's footpads regularly for signs of abrasion, foreign bodies, tears, or blistering from hot pavement. Leave your dog at home in hot weather. Dogs are unable to cool themselves through sweating, and heatstroke in jogging dogs is a common emergency seen by veterinarians in the summer. In winter, check between the pads for balls of ice (coating the paws with Vaseline can help keep the ice balls down somewhat), and rinse the feet when returning from walking on rock salt.

## Water

Swimming is an excellent exercise, especially in the summer or for dogs with arthritis or other injuries. Most JRTs take right to the water,

*The JRT's innate urge to explore tight places starts early:*

but if you have one that needs a little coaxing, get right in the water with him and ease him in gradually. Support his rear end so that he doesn't splash on top of the water, and you will soon have a JRT swimmer on your hands.

### Basic Instinct

Some JRT owners encourage their dogs to follow their instincts and hunt. Barns may harbor a bevy of rats that your terrier may be able to seek and destroy. Always beware that many holes that attract small mammals also attract snakes, some of which may be poisonous. Rat bites, too, can pose a danger. If your heart is set on hunting larger game, be aware that in the United States it is illegal to hunt fur-bearing animals in their dens. Most JRT owners find that terrier trials are the best way to satisfy their terrier's love of the hunt.

## Trials and Tribulations

Perhaps because JRTs think just about anything that involves movement is great fun, the list of organized activities available to them is extensive. AKC and JRTCA sponsored competitions include conformation, obedience, agility, earthdog, and tracking, and the JRTCA (but not AKC) also offers racing, high jump, and water races.

**Earthdog (or in JRTCA, go-to-ground) events** are traditionally the most important of the competitions. In these trials, terriers must enter a man-made but natural-appearing tunnel, at the end of which are caged animals (usually rats). Dogs are expected to enter the hole without hesitation, traverse the tunnel, and work the quarry by barking, digging, growling, and whining.

Terrier trials are also sponsored by the American Working Terrier Association (AWTA). The Novice class consists of a 10-foot-long (3.1-m) tunnel with one turn. The dog is released 10 feet from the tunnel entrance, and is given one minute to traverse the tunnel and begin working the caged rats. Working should continue for 30 seconds, after which the dog is lifted out of a trapdoor. The handler can help direct the dog to the entrance and encourage him to work the rat, but such help will result in a nonqualifying score. Training runs are also held after the end of most trials, using wooden above-ground tunnels.

**Racing** is the most popular and spectacular of JRT competitions. JRTCA-sanctioned trials may either be run on a flat track or over four to six low hurdles (not over 8 inches (20 cm) for pups, or 16 inches (40.6 cm) for adults), over a distance of 150 to 240 feet (45.7–73.2 m). The track is about 6 to 8 feet (1.8–2.4 m) wide and fenced, with a catch area behind the finish. Dogs are divided according to age and height (over and under 12½ inches (31.8 cm), but still within the JRTCA standard of 10 to 15 inches (25–38 cm)). You should get a JRTCA height card when your dog reaches 18 months of age. This is an official recording of your dog's height as measured by conformation judges.

**Conformation** competition is similar to that at any dog show, with each dog evaluated in comparison to the standard of perfection. Type and soundness, with an emphasis on the struc-

*Hunting underground comes naturally to a JRT, and go-to-ground and earthdog trials let them show off their skills under controlled circumstances.*

ture necessary to do the job of a working JRT, are paramount. Dogs should be trained to trot smartly beside you on lead, and to stand at attention, with legs parallel to each other and front legs and rear hocks perpendicular to the ground. Discreet use of a squeaky toy, piece of fur, or liver is helpful in focusing the dog's attention and keeping him alert in the ring. Keep your Jack happy so that he doesn't let his tail drop while in the ring. Note that unlike many terrier breeds, JRTs are never sparred (faced off to each other to show gameness).

**Obedience** trials start with fairly simple requirements and progress to very difficult ones. The lowest level of AKC trials, called Novice, requires the dog to:

✔ Heel on lead, sitting automatically each time you stop, negotiating right, left, and about turns without guidance from you, and changing to a faster and slower pace;

✔ Heel in a figure 8 around two people, still on lead;

✔ Stand still off lead 6 feet away from you and allow a judge to touch him.

✔ Do the exercises in the first step, except off lead;

✔ Come to you when called from 20 feet (6 m) away, and then return to heel position on command;

✔ Stay in a sitting position with a group of other dogs, while you are 20 feet (6 m) away, for one minute; and

✔ Stay in a down position with the same group while you are 20 feet (6 m) away, for three minutes.

Open (CDX) exercises include more advanced exercises and require retrieving and jumping. Utility (UD) requires scent discrimination, and directed retrieving and jumping. The supreme obedience title is the Obedience Trial Champion (OTCh), awarded only to dogs with UDs that outscore many other UD dogs in many, many trials.

JRTCA trial requirements may vary from trial to trial, but are generally not unlike AKC trials.

**Agility** competition requires a combination of obedience and athleticism, all of which adds up to a lot of fun and excitement! Dogs traverse tunnels, ramps, teeter-totters, and hurdles, with various levels of difficulty. JRTs love the challenge and are among the most agile of dogs. JRTCA awards, in increasing level of difficulty, agility certificates I, II, and III. The AKC awards, in increasing level of difficulty, the titles Novice Agility Dog (NAD), Open Agility Dog (CAD), Agility Dog Excellent (ADE), and Master Agility Excellent (MAX). It also awards titles for competitions called "Jumpers With Weaves," which emphasizes speed and jumping over control and precision.

Agility classes for all breeds are springing up in larger cities throughout the country, and you may be able to find a group in your area. If not, you can improvise your own set of obstacles in your backyard. Entice your dog to walk through a tunnel made of sheets draped over chairs; guide him with treats to weave in and out of a series of poles made from several plumber's helpers placed in line; make him comfortable walking on a wide raised board; and teach him to jump through a tire and over a hurdle.

**Tracking** is an AKC competition requiring the dog to follow a human scent trail. A dog can earn the AKC Tracking Dog (TD) title by following a 440- to 500-yard (402–457-m) track with three to five turns laid by a person from 30 minutes to 2 hours before. A Tracking Dog Excellent (TDX) title is earned by following an "older" (three to five hours) and longer (800 to 1,000-yard) (731.5–914.4-m) track with five to seven turns and more challenging circumstances. One of these circumstances is the existence of cross-tracks laid by another tracklayer about 1½ hours after the first track was laid. In addition, the actual track may cross various types of terrain and obstacles, including plowed land, woods, streams, bridges, and lightly traveled roads. A dog can earn the Variable Surface Tracking (VST) title by following a three- to five-hour track, 600 to 800

*Layout for go-to-ground competition.*

*Racing is the most popular—and fun—of the competitions.*

yards (548.6–731.5 m) long, over a variety of surfaces, such as might be normally encountered when tracking in the real world. At least three different surface areas are included, of which at least one must include vegetation and at least two must be devoid of vegetation (for example, sand or concrete).

**Trailing and locating** is a JRTCA competition that requires dogs to follow a scent through a short tunnel and an open area to locate a simulated quarry. Start with very short trails, gradually working backwards, further from the quarry. JRTs are natural sniffers, and most catch on quickly as long as it leads to fun. Incidentally, if your JRT is adept at this,

and you want to provide a real service to the community, you might consider search-and-rescue training, where dogs use their noses (and other senses) to find lost people or bodies. The ever ready and versatile JRT is a natural at this most rewarding endeavor.

*Just follow your nose...to a tracking title!*

# INFORMATION

**Organizations**
(Note that addresses may change.)

The Jack Russell Terrier Club of America, Inc.
P.O. Box 4527
Lutherville, MD 21094-4527
(410) 561-3655
http://www.terrier.com/index.php3

The Jack Russell Terrier Association of America
Maria Sacco, Secretary
P.O. Box 3223
Alexandria, VA 22302
E-mail: jrtaa@usa.net
http://www.jrtaa.org/
P.O. Box 115
Winchester Center, CT 06094
(203) 379-3282

The Jack Russell Terrier Club of Canada
Yvonne Downey
242 Henrietta Street
Fort Erie, Ontario L2A 2K7
Canada
(905) 871-8691

The Jack Russell Terrier Club of Great Britain
Chairperson: Greg Mousley
Aston Heath Farm
Sudbury, Derbyshire DEG S88
England

The English Jack Russell Terrier Club Alliance
P.O. Box 294129
Phelan, CA 92329-4129
E-mail: shortyjrt@ejrtca.com
http://www.ejrtca.com

The American Working Terrier Association
Patricia Adams Lent
503 NC 55 West
Mt. Olive, NC 28465
http://www.dirt-dog.com/awta/index.shtml

AKC Earthdog Clubs
http://www.akc.org/dic/clubs/other/earthcb.cfm

American Kennel Club (AKC)
5580 Centerview Drive
Raleigh, NC 27606-3390
(919) 233-9767
E-mail: info@akc.org
http://www.akc.org/

JRTCA Russell Rescue
Catherine Romaine Brown
P.O. Box 24
Geneseo, NY 14454-9731
(716) 226-2826
E-mail: brownacorn@aol.com
http://www.terrier.com/rescue/contacts.php3

JRTAA Rescue
Karyn Collins
(860) 445-1390
E-mail: Karyn4Dave@aol.com

Orthopedic Foundation for Animals (OFA)
2300 Nifong Boulevard
Columbia, MO 65201
(573) 442-0418
E-mail: ofa@offa.org
http://www.offa.org/

Canine Eye Registration Foundation (CERF)
South Campus Courts C
Purdue University
West Lafayette, IN 47906

Home Again Microchip Service
1-800-LONELY-ONE

**Magazines**
*True Grit*
Official publication of the JRTCA

*JRTAA Newsletter*
Official publication of the JRTAA

*Down to Earth*
Official publication of the AWTA

*AKC Gazette* (covers general aspects of all
  breeds)
AKC Order Desk
5580 Centerview Drive
Raleigh, NC 27606-3390
(919) 233-9767; E-mail: *orderdesk@akc.org*
*http://www.akc.org/insideAKC/resources/subs.cfm*

*Dog Fancy*
P.O. Box 53264
Boulder, CO 80322-3264
(303) 666-8504

*Dog World*
500 N. Dearborn, Suite 1100
Chicago, IL 60610
(312) 396-0600
E-mail: *Info@dogworldmag.com*
*http://www.dogworldmag.com/*

**Books**
Atter, Sheila. *Jack Russell Terriers Today.* Glous-
  estershire, Great Britain: Ringpress Books,
  Ltd., 1995.
Britt-Hay, Deborah. *The Complete Idiot's Guide
  to Owning, Raising, and Training a Jack Rus-
  sell Terrier.* New York, NY: Howell Book
  House, 1999.

Chapman, Eddie. *The Working Jack Russell
  Terrier.* Dorchester, Great Britain: Henry King
  at the Dorset Press, 1985.
Coile, D. Caroline. *Encyclopedia of Dog Breeds.*
  Hauppauge, NY: Barron's Educational Series,
  Inc., 1998.
____. *Show Me! A dog showing primer.* Haup-
  pauge, NY: Barron's Educational Series, Inc.,
  1997.
____. *The Jack Russell Terrier Handbook.* Haup-
  pauge, NY: Barron's Educational Series, Inc.,
  2000.
Frier-Murza, Jo Ann. *Earthdog Ins and Outs.*
  Centreville, AL: OTR Publications, 1999.
Jackson, Jean and Frank. *The Making of the
  Parson Jack Russell Terrier.* Dover, NH: The
  Boydell Press, 1986.
____. *Parson Jack Russell Terriers: An Owner's
  Companion.* London, England: The Crowood
  Press, 1990.
____. *The Parson and Jack Russell Terriers.*
  London, England: Popular Dogs Publishing
  Co., Ltd., 1991.
Lent, Patricia. *Sport With Terriers.* Rome, NY:
  Arner Publications, 1973.
Strom, Mary. *The Ultimate Jack Russell Terrier.*
  New York, NY: Howell Book House, 1999.

# I N D E X

## About the Author

D. Caroline Coile is an award-winning author who has written 14 books and over 100 articles about dogs for both scientific and lay publications. She holds a Ph.D. in the field of neuroscience and behavior, with special interests in canine sensory systems, genetics, and behavior. Her dogs have been nationally ranked in conformation, obedience, and field-trial competition.

## Photo Credits

Isabelle Francais: pages 2–3, 6, 8, 10, 12, 19, 27, 28, 33, 34, 38, 48, 54, 58, 77, 82, 90, 98; Tara Darling: pages 4, 45, 78, 107 top; Kent and Donna Dannen: pages 9, 65, 107 bottom; Toni Tucker: page 7, 72, 73; Elizabeth Flynn: pages 14, 40, 47, 50, 53, 71, 84, 104; Sharon Eide: pages 11, 17, 20, 24, 31, 32, 43, 44, 61, 62, 64, 68, 74, 86, 105, 109; Judith Strom: pages 23, 80; Bonnie Nance: pages 36, 57, 76, 83, 88; Pets by Paulette: pages 39, 60, 70, 95, 102.

## Cover Credits

Front cover: Pets by Paulette; Inside front cover, inside back cover, back cover: Isabelle Francais.

### Important Note

This pet owner's guide tells the reader how to buy or adopt, and care for a Jack Russell Terrier. The author and the publisher consider it important to point out that the advice given in the book is meant primarily for normally developed dogs of excellent physical health and good character.

Anyone who adopts a fully grown dog should be aware that the animal has already formed its basic impressions of human beings. The new owner should watch the animal carefully, including its behavior toward humans, and should meet the previous owner.

If the dog comes from a shelter, it may be possible to get some information on the dog's background and peculiarities there. There are dogs that, as a result of bad experiences with humans, behave in an unnatural manner or may even bite. Only people that have experience with dogs should take in such animals.

Caution is further advised in the association of children with dogs, in meeting with other dogs, and in exercising the dog without a leash.

Even well-behaved and carefully supervised dogs sometimes do damage to someone else's property or cause accidents. It is therefore in the owner's interest to be adequately insured against such eventualities, and we strongly urge all dog owners to purchase a liability policy that covers their dog.

## Acknowledgments

The information contained in this book comes from a variety of sources: breeders, original research, scientific articles, and veterinary journals. But by far my most heartfelt gratitude must go to my most demanding teachers, who have taught me the skills of both home repair and dog repair, and whetted my curiosity (and carpets) about everything canine for the past 30 years: Baha, Khyber, Tundra, Kara, Hypatia, Savannah, Sissy, Dixie, Bobby, Kitty, Jeepers, Beanie, Junior, Khyzi, Wolfman, Stinky, Omen, Isis, Minka, Honey, and Luna.

Breed standards are reprinted courtesy of the JRTAA and AKC.

*All inquiries should be addressed to:*
Barron's Educational Series, Inc.
250 Wireless Boulevard
Hauppauge, NY 11788
**http://www.barronseduc.com**

International Standard Book No. 0-7641-1048-9

*Library of Congress Catalog Card No. 99-59660*

**Library of Congress Cataloging-in-Publication Data**
Coile, D. Caroline.
   Jack Russell terriers : everything about purchase, care, nutrition, behavior, and training / D. Caroline Coile.—2nd ed.
      p.   cm. — (A Complete pet owner's manual)
   Includes bibliographical references.
   ISBN 0-7641-1048-9 (alk. paper)
   1. Jack Russell terrier. I. Title. II. Series.
SF429.J27 C65      2000
636.755—dc21                                    99-59660
                                                            CIP

Printed in Hong Kong
9 8 7